Oxford excellence for the Caribbean

STP Caribbean Mathematics

FOURTH EDITION

Workbook 2

S Chandler
E Smith

OXFORD

Contents

Answers to the questions in this book can be found on your free support website. Access your support website here: **www.oxfordsecondary.com/9780198426561**

1 Working with numbers

In questions **1** to **12**, choose the letter that gives the correct answer.

1 a and b are odd numbers and $a + b = c$. So, c is:

   A an even number

   B an odd number

   C the inverse of a under addition

   D a fraction smaller than 1

2 Expressed to two significant figures, $6.7483 =$

   A 6.7

   B 6.74

   C 6.75

   D 6.8

3 5.5% as a decimal is:

   A 0.055

   B 0.55

   C 5.5

   D 55

4 0.07 as a percentage is:

   A 0.07%

   B 0.7%

   C 7%

   D 70%

5 $\dfrac{7}{20}$ as a decimal is:

   A 0.7

   B 0.07

   C 0.035

   D 0.35

6 The inverse of 7 under addition is:

   A -7

   B 0

   C $\dfrac{1}{7}$

   D 7

7 The inverse of 7 under multiplication is:

   A -7

   B 0

   C $\dfrac{1}{7}$

   D 7

8 $9 + 0 = 9$ so 0 is:

   A the inverse of 9 under addition

   B the identity element for addition

   C not a member of the set of integers

   D the inverse of 9 under multiplication

9 The inverse of 3 under addition is:

   A 3

   B $\dfrac{1}{3}$

   C 0

   D -3

10 As a single expression in index form, $2^9 \div 2^5$ is:

   A 2^9

   B 2^5

   C 2^4

   D 2^3

11 p is an even number, q is an odd number and $r = p + q$. So, r is:

A the identity element under addition

B the inverse of q under addition

C an odd number

D an even number

12 In standard form, the number $734\,000\,000$ is:

A 7.34×10^6

B 7.34×10^7

C 7.34×10^8

D 7.34×10^9

13 p, q and r are integers. Which of the following statements are true?

a $p - q = q - p$ _____

b $p + q = q + p$ _____

c $p + q$ is an integer _____

d $p + q \times r = p \times r + q$ _____

14 p and q are integers and $p + q = r$.

State whether or not each of these statements must be true:

a r is an integer _____

b r is an odd integer _____

c r is a fraction smaller than 1

_____

d r is the identity element under addition.

_____

15 Work out each fraction as a decimal:

a $\dfrac{4}{5}$ _____

b $\dfrac{5}{8}$ _____

c $\dfrac{7}{10}$ _____

d $\dfrac{1}{8}$ _____

e $\dfrac{8}{25}$ _____

16 Work out each fraction as a decimal:

a $\dfrac{2}{5}$ _____

b $\dfrac{7}{20}$ _____

c $\dfrac{9}{10}$ _____

d $\dfrac{3}{8}$ _____

17 Write each decimal as a fraction in its lowest terms, using mixed numbers where necessary:

a 0.04 _____

b 18.5 _____

c 2.25 _____

d 8.02 _____

e 0.06 _____

18 Write each decimal as a fraction in its lowest terms, using mixed numbers where necessary:

a 0.8 _____

b 0.05 _____

c 3.02 _____

d 4.75 _____

19 Write these decimals as percentages:

   a 0.8   _____

   b 0.055   _____

   c 0.45   _____

   d 1.6   _____

   e 8.25   _____

20 Write these decimals as percentages:

   a 0.6   _____

   b 0.045   _____

   c 0.375   _____

   d 0.55   _____

   e 1.8   _____

   f 5.5   _____

21 Express each percentage as a decimal:

   a 14%   _____

   b 35.5%   _____

   c 4.4%   _____

   d 270%   _____

22 Write these percentages as decimals:

   a 90%   _____

   b 15.5%   _____

   c 3.3%   _____

   d 170%   _____

23 Express each fraction as a percentage:

   a $\frac{11}{20}$ _____

   b $\frac{47}{50}$ _____

   c $\frac{56}{80}$ _____

   d $\frac{27}{40}$ _____

24 Write each percentage as a fraction in its lowest terms:

   a 80%   _____

   b 46%   _____

   c 24%   _____

   d 95%   _____

25 Express each fraction as a percentage:

   a $\frac{9}{20}$ _____

   b $\frac{37}{50}$ _____

   c $\frac{25}{40}$ _____

   d $\frac{28}{50}$ _____

26 Two oranges in a bag of eight oranges are bad.

   Express the number of bad oranges as:

   a a fraction   _____

   b a percentage _____

   c a decimal.   _____

27 The cost of running a car is 28% fuel, $\frac{7}{20}$ tax and insurance, and the remainder depreciation.

   a What fraction of the running cost is fuel?

   _____

   b What percentage of the running cost is tax and insurance? _____

   c What percentage is depreciation?

   _____

28 Calculate:

a $3 \times (-4)$ _____

b $5 - (-3)$ _____

c $(-60) \div (-20)$ _____

d $(-8) \div (-16)$ _____

29 Calculate:

a $4(6-2) - 4(5-4)$ _____

b $10 - 3(13 - 10)$ _____

c $6 \times 9 - 2(9 - 18)$ _____

30 Calculate:

a $(-4 \div 8) \times 2$ _____

b $\dfrac{5-11}{3-5}$ _____

c $\dfrac{2 \times (17-6)}{(9+13) \times (-3)}$ _____

31 Write in standard form:

a 243.2 _____

b $57\,300$ _____

c $426\,000$ _____

32 Calculate:

a $\dfrac{8 \times (-4) \times (7-3)}{2 \times (-12)}$ _____

b $\dfrac{(-12) \times 3 \times (-8)}{4 \times (-16)}$ _____

33 Which law, if any, (associative, commutative or distributive) does each of the following statements illustrate?

a $8 + 15 = 15 + 8$ _____

b $5 \times (3+4) = 5 \times 3 + 5 \times 4$ _____

c $7 + 4 + 8 = 8 + 4 + 7$ _____

d $8 \times 9 = 9 \times 8$ _____

e $4 \times (5-2) = 4 \times 5 + 4 \times (-2)$ _____

f $6 \times (5 \times 2) = (6 \times 5) \times 2$ _____

g $(8+3) + 5 = 8 + (3+5)$ _____

34 Which law (associative, commutative or distributive), if any, does each of the following statements illustrate?

a $5 + 7 = 7 + 5$ _____

b $6 \times (2+5) = 6 \times 2 + 6 \times 5$

_____

c $9 \times 6 = 6 \times 9$ _____

d $4 \times (5-3) = 4 \times 5 - 4 \times 3$

_____

e $9 + 5 + 3 = 3 + 5 + 9$ _____

35 Simplify:

a $a^7 \div a^5$ _____

b $\dfrac{a^5 \times a^7}{a^4}$ _____

36 Find:

a 5^2 _____

b 7^3 _____

c 2^4 _____

d 4^3 _____

37 Find the value of:

a 5.9×10^2 _____

b 3.42×10^1 _____

c 7.46×10^3 _____

d 1.64×10^4 _____

38 Express as a single expression in index form:

a $2^3 \times 2^4 =$ _____

b $5^4 \times 5^5 =$ _____

c $s^3 \times s^5 =$ _____

d $p^5 \times p^5 =$ _____

39 Express as a single expression in index form:

a $2^6 \div 2^4 =$ _____

b $5^4 \div 5^3 =$ _____

c $a^8 \div a^5 =$ _____

d $q^{10} \div q^7 =$ _____

e $2^3 \times 2^4 \times 2^5 =$ _____

f $3^4 \times 3^7 \div 3^3 =$ _____

g $r^5 \div r^4 \times r^3 =$ _____

40 Find the value of:

a 3^{-1} _____

b 12^{-1} _____

c 6^{-3} _____

d 7^{-3} _____

e 5^{-2} _____

41 Find the value of:

a 5.4×10^{-1} _____

b 27.6×10^{-1} _____

c 3.25×10^{-3} _____

d 71×10^{-3} _____

e 8.22×10^{-2} _____

f 3.354×10^{-4} _____

g 1.7979×10^3 _____

42 Express as a single number (or expression) in index form:

a $2^6 \div 2^8 =$ _____

b $3^4 \div 3^5 =$ _____

c $x^2 \div x^5 =$ _____

d $p^3 \div p^7 =$ _____

43 Find the value of:

a 8^2 _____

b 6^0 _____

c 7^{-1} _____

d 4.51×10^2 _____

44 Write as a single expression in index form:

a $3^3 \times 3^4$ _____

b $2^4 \times 2^0 \times 2^5$ _____

c $2^{-2} \times 2^4$ _____

d $b^4 \div b^4$ _____

e $c^6 \div c^2$ _____

f $a^3 \times a^2 \div a^5$ _____

g $\dfrac{3^2 \times 3^5}{3^4}$ _____

h $\dfrac{b^4 \times b^0}{b^3}$ _____

45 Write each of the following numbers as ordinary numbers:

a 2.22×10^4 _____

b 5.73×10^{-2} _____

c 7.44×10^{-5} _____

d 6.21×10^{-4} _____

e 6.782×10^{-2} _____

f 3.76×10^8 _____

46 Write the following numbers in standard form:

a   3600   _____

b   7 050 887   _____

c   0.076   _____

d   0.000 08   _____

e   72   _____

f   0.000 000 000 054   _____

g   37 000 000 000   _____

h   854   _____

47 Round:

a   75 643 to the nearest 100

_____

b   649 to the nearest 10   _____

c   237 563 to the nearest 100

_____

d   8767 to the nearest 1000

_____

e   7664 to the nearest 10   _____

f   194 500 to the nearest 1000

_____

48 Give each number correct to the number of decimal places given in the brackets:

a   7.07 (1)   _____

b   0.048 (2)   _____

c   64.46 (1)   _____

d   0.006 74 (4)   _____

e   0.436 78 (3)   _____

f   0.899 72 (2)   _____

49 For each number write down the significant figure specified in the bracket:

a   93.45 (1st)   _____

b   0.008 76 (2nd)   _____

c   4.3876 (3rd)   _____

d   56 731 (4th)   _____

e   3.726 (2nd)   _____

f   5.0367 (3rd)   _____

50 Give each number correct to the number of significant figures indicated in the bracket:

a   4589 (1)   _____

b   666 (2)   _____

c   0.065 89 (3)   _____

d   0.705 783 3 (4)   _____

e   345.65 (3)   _____

f   176.5436 (2)   _____

51 Give, correct to 2 s.f.:

a $20 \div 7$ _____

b $34 \div 6$ _____

c $64 \div 3$ _____

d $136 \div 9$ _____

e $0.82 \div 5$ _____

f $243 \div 8$ _____

52 Give each number to 1 s.f. and hence find a rough answer for each of the following:

a 3.94×24.7 _____

b 0.42×58.6 _____

c $976 \div 49.3$ _____

d 0.0056×0.0824 _____

e $7.46 \div 6.88$ _____

f $1109 \div 98$ _____

g $\dfrac{6.23 \times 3.88}{1.97}$ _____

h $\dfrac{856 \times 0.092}{9.197}$ _____

i $\dfrac{0.175 \times 5.28}{0.531}$ _____

j $\dfrac{78.37 \times 0.0884}{5.87}$ _____

53 Make a rough estimate of the answer, then use your calculator to give the answer correct to 3 s.f.:

a 3.56×2.07 _____

b 2.223×4.043 _____

c $8.421 \div 5.784$ _____

d 756×0.867 _____

e $573.4 \div 37.6$ _____

f $3000 \div 27.45$ _____

54 Make a rough estimate of the answer, then use your calculator to give the answer correct to 3 s.f.:

a $(0.46)^2$ _____

b 0.00735×4.633 _____

c $63.4 \div 584$ _____

d $0.678 \div 0.736$ _____

e $0.524 \div 6.049$ _____

f $4000 \div 64.9$ _____

Write in figures the numbers represented by the markers in questions **1** to **4**.

	5^4	5^3	5^2	5	Units
1			$\vdots$		$\vdots$
2			$\cdot$	$\cdot$	$\vdots$
3	$\cdot$	$\vdots$	$\vdots$	$\cdot$	
4	$\vdots$	$\vdots$		$\cdot$	

1 _____ **2** _____ **3** _____ **4** _____

5 Write the following numbers in headed columns:

  a 425   **b** 3305

  c 2025   **d** 10345

	5^4	5^3	5^2	5	Units
a					
b					
c					
d					

6 Write the following numbers as denary numbers, i.e. to base 10:

  a 23_5 _____

  b 41_5 _____

  c 203_5 _____

  d 310_5 _____

7 Write the following numbers in base 5:

  a 9_{10} _____

  b 14_{10} _____

  c 11_{10} _____

  d 32_{10} _____

  e 73_{10} _____

  f 200_{10} _____

In questions **8** to **14**, write the numbers:

  a in headed columns

  b as denary numbers.

8 22_4 **a**

    b _____

9 23_5 **a**

    b _____

10 153_7 **a**

    b _____

11 304_5 **a**

    b _____

12 267_8 **a**

    b _____

13 1010_6 **a**

    b _____

14 1121_3 **a**

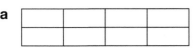

    b _____

15 Write the following denary numbers to the base given in brackets:

a 12 (4) _____

b 23 (6) _____

c 34 (5) _____

d 54 (8) _____

e 74 (6) _____

f 52 (7) _____

g 50 (4) _____

16 Write the following denary numbers to the base given in brackets:

a 147 (8) _____

b 133 (5) _____

c 343 (5) _____

d 294 (6) _____

e 314 (8) _____

f 273 (7) _____

g 79 (3) _____

17 Find:

a $12_3 + 12_3$ _____

b $34_5 + 42_5$ _____

c $25_6 + 52_6$ _____

d $101_2 + 110_2$ _____

e $225_6 + 403_6$ _____

f $121_3 + 221_3$ _____

g $11011_2 + 10101_2$ _____

18 Find:

a $30_5 - 11_5$ _____

b $333_4 - 201_4$ _____

c $103_6 - 35_6$ _____

d $10100_2 - 1101_2$ _____

e $231_4 - 133_4$ _____

f $1000_3 - 101_3$ _____

g $253_8 - 226_8$ _____

19 Find:

a $3_5 \times 3_5$ _____

b $2_4 \times 2_4$ _____

c $3_6 \times 4_6$ _____

d $34_7 \times 3_7$ _____

e $212_3 \times 2_3$ _____

f $314_5 \times 2_5$ _____

g $321_4 \times 3_4$ _____

20 Find:

a $344_6 + 213_6$ _____

b $212_5 \times 4_5$ _____

c $127_8 + 355_8$ _____

d $535_6 - 444_6$ _____

e $32_5 \times 4_5$ _____

f $231_5 - 124_5$ _____

g $33_4 \times 3_4$ _____

21 Find:

a $121_4 + 23_4$ _____

b $62_8 + 24_8$ _____

c $134_5 + 43_5$ _____

d $2021_3 + 210_3$ _____

e $1101_2 + 1011_2$ _____

f $447_8 + 53_8$ _____

g $221_3 + 22221_3$ _____

22 Find:

   a $235_8 + 6_8$ ———————————

   b $542_8 + 5_8$ ———————————

   c $532_7 + 5_7$ ———————————

23 Find:

   a $341_5 - 3_5$ ———————————

   b $421_5 - 4_5$ ———————————

   c $352_6 - 5_6$ ———————————

24 Find:

   a $134_5 + 23_5$ ———————————

   b $124_5 - 31_5$ ———————————

   c $232_5 \times 12_5$ ———————————

25 Express the following numbers, which are to the base 8, as denary numbers:

   a 23_8 ———————————

   b 542_8 ———————————

   c 267_8 ———————————

   d 534_8 ———————————

26 Express the following numbers, which are to the base 4, as denary numbers:

   a 32_4 ———————————

   b 123_4 ———————————

   c 322_4 ———————————

   d 1232_4 ———————————

27 Find:

   a $213_5 - 34_5$ ———————————

   b $374_8 + 166_8$ ———————————

   c $525_8 - 266$ ———————————

28 Convert the following denary numbers into binary numbers:

   a 9   ———————————

   b 11   ———————————

   c 17   ———————————

   d 27   ———————————

29 Convert the following binary numbers into denary numbers:

   a 110   ———————————

   b 111   ———————————

   c 1101   ———————————

   d 10101   ———————————

30 Which is the larger of the following pairs of binary numbers?

   a 110, 101   ———————————

   b 1011, 1100   ———————————

   c 10101, 1111   ———————————

31 Which is the largest of the following binary numbers?

   a 1010, 111, 1001   ———————————

   b 11000, 10100, 10011   ———————————

32 Which of these binary numbers are odd numbers?

   1001, 1100, 10001, 110   ———————————

33 Which of these binary numbers are even numbers?

   100, 1100, 10001, 11   ———————————

34 How many digits are there in 4^3 written in base 4?

   ———————————

35 Convert the following denary numbers to base 4 numbers:

a 9 _____

b 15 _____

c 24 _____

36 Find:

a $132_4 \times 32_4$ _____

b $314_5 \times 42_5$ _____

c $63_8 \times 36_8$ _____

37 a Find $37_8 \times 62_8$ as a number to base 8.

_____

b Express 37_8 and 62_8 as denary numbers.

$37_8 =$ _____

$62_8 =$ _____

c Multiply together your answers to **b**.

_____

d Change your answer to **c** to base 8.

Does it agree with your answer to part **a**?

_____

38 a Find $35_6 \times 52_6$ as a number to base 6.

_____

b Express 35_6 and 52_6 as denary numbers.

_____

c Multiply together your two answers for **b**.

_____

d Change your answer to **c** into a number to base 6.

_____

e Does this answer agree with your answer to **a**?

_____

39 Find $56_7 \times 34_7$ using the process described in question **38** as a check on your working.

_____

_____

_____

40 Find $33_4 \times 22_4$ and use the process described in question **38** as a check on your working.

_____

_____

_____

41 Write the following numbers as denary numbers:

a 13_4 _____

b 1011_2 _____

c 432_5 _____

42 Find the bases in which the following calculations have been done:

a $34 + 15 = 53$ _____

b $13 - 4 = 7$ _____

c $13 \times 3 = 111$ _____

43 Find:

a $1011_2 + 1100_2$ _____

b $101_2 + 111_2$ _____

c $11101_2 - 111_2$ _____

d $1111_2 \times 1011_2$ _____

e $10101_2 + 1111_2$ _____

f $10101_2 - 1111_2$ _____

g $11011_2 \times 1101_2$ _____

3 Algebra

In questions **1** to **7**, choose the letter that gives the correct answer.

1 The value of x that satisfies the equation $2x - 3 = 5$ is:

A 0

B 1

C 2

D 4

2 The value of x that satisfies the equation $7x - 3 = 4x + 9$ is

A 1

B 2

C 3

D 4

3 When simplified, $3x - 4(x - 1) =$

A $4 - x$

B $7x + 4$

C $4 + x$

D $4 - 2x$

4 When simplified, $8 - 3(x - 2) =$

A $5x - 10$

B $14 - 3x$

C $6 - 3x$

D $5x - 2$

5 The value of x that satisfies the equation $\frac{x}{3} = -2$ is:

A -6

B -1

C 1

D 6

6 Given that $p = q - 3r$, if $q = 5$, $r = -2$, then $p =$

A 11

B 9

C 1

D -4

7 When simplified, $2(3x - 5) - 4(x - 3) =$

A $2x - 22$

B $10x + 2$

C $2x + 2$

D $2x - 2$

8 Solve the following equations:

a $3x = 12$ $x =$ _____

b $x - 4 = 2$ $x =$ _____

c $3x + 4 = 10$ $x =$ _____

d $2 + 3x = 11$ $x =$ _____

e $4 + 8x = 20$ $x =$ _____

f $5x - 3 = 12$ $x =$ _____

Solve the following equations:

9 a $10x = 0$ _____

b $2x - 10 = 8$ _____

c $4x - 13 = 3$ _____

10 a $3x - 9 = 0$ _____

b $12x = -48$ _____

c $7x = -84$ _____

11 a $14x = 21$ _____

b $2x - 5 = 7$ _____

c $5x - 9 = 21$ _____

12 Solve the following equations:

  a $3x + 4 = 2x + 9$ $x =$ _____

  b $x - 7 = 5 - x$ $x =$ _____

  c $x + 3 = 4x$ $x =$ _____

  d $3 - 3x = 7 - x$ $x =$ _____

  e $2x + 2 + 3x = 12$ $x =$ _____

  f $5 + x - 3 = 3x$ $x =$ _____

13 Solve the following equations:

  a $x + 18 = 4x + 3$ $x =$ _____

  b $3x + 5 = 7x - 3$ $x =$ _____

  c $2x + 15 = 5x - 6$ $x =$ _____

  d $13 - 3z = 1 + z$ $z =$ _____

  e $2y + 7 = 5y + 4$ $y =$ _____

  f $6x + 59 = 13x + 17$ $x =$ _____

14 a $-4x = 8$ _____

  b $2x + 5 = x + 9$ _____

  c $5x + 4 = 3x + 12$ _____

15 a $19 - 5x = 6$ _____

  b $-2x = -10$ _____

  c $7x - 3 = -31$ _____

16 a $6 - 3x = 6$ _____

  b $-3x - 5 = 4$ _____

  c $2x + 5 = x + 9$ _____

17 a $5x + 4 = 3x + 12$ _____

  b $7x - 3 = 4x + 15$ _____

18 Simplify:

  a $3(x + 2) + 4$ _____

  b $5x + 4(x + 1)$ _____

  c $2(3x - 4) + 3(x + 1)$ _____

  d $8(3 - x) + 4(2 + 4x)$ _____

  e $6(3 - x) + 2(1 - 3x)$ _____

  f $7(2 + 3x) + 3(2x - 4)$ _____

19 Simplify:

  a $5(x + 4) + 2(2x + 3)$ _____

  b $2(3x - 3) + 3(x - 4)$ _____

  c $3(x + 5) + 2(2x + 5)$ _____

  d $6(2x + 3) + 3(2x + 3)$ _____

  e $2(x - 6) + 4(2x + 6)$ _____

  f $4(4x + 2) + 5(2x - 4)$ _____

20 Simplify:

  a $6(2 - x) + 3(1 - x)$ _____

  b $3(3 + 2x) + 2(4 + x)$ _____

  c $2(5 - 3x) + 5(3 + 3x)$ _____

  d $3(2 + 2x) + 4(2 - x)$ _____

  e $5(4 - 5x) + 3(5 - 4x)$ _____

  f $4(6 + x) + 7(1 + 7x)$ _____

21 Solve the following equations:

  a $2(x + 2) = 10$ _____

  b $2(3x - 1) = 10$ _____

  c $3(3x - 7) = 2x + 7$ _____

  d $6(x - 2) = 3x + 6$ _____

  e $10(x - 2) = 5$ _____

  f $3(1 + 2x) = 9$ _____

22 Solve the following equations:

   a $5(2x - 1) - 44 = 14$ ———————

   b $2(2x - 7) = 6$ ———————

   c $5(x - 1) + 3 = 8$ ———————

   d $2(3x - 1) - 3 = 13$ ———————

   e $3 + 2(3x + 4) = 41$ ———————

   f $3(3x + 7) - 17 = 28$ ———————

   g $6(4x - 5) + 9 = 51$ ———————

23 Simplify:

   a $(+4) \times (-3)$ ———————

   b $(-7) \times (-5)$ ———————

   c $(+6) \times \left(-\dfrac{1}{3}\right)$ ———————

   d $\left(\dfrac{1}{4}\right) \div \left(-\dfrac{1}{2}\right)$ ———————

   e $(-8) \div (-4)$ ———————

24 Simplify:

   a $10 - 3(x - 3)$ ———————

   b $5x + 2(3x - 1)$ ———————

   c $3x - 3(4 - 5x)$ ———————

   d $3(x + 2) - (x + 7)$ ———————

   e $8(x - 3) + 3(2x - 1)$ ———————

   f $7(2x - 3) - 5(x - 2)$ ———————

25 Solve the following equations:

   a $5(x - 1) = 2(x + 8)$ ———————

   b $4(3 - x) = 3(x + 4)$ ———————

   c $3(x - 4) = x + 12$ ———————

   d $7(5 - x) = 2(3x - 2)$ ———————

   e $2(x + 4) = 3(2x + 1)$ ———————

   f $5(x + 2) - 4 = 2(x + 5)$ ———————

26 I think of a number, halve it and add 3. The result is 12. What was the number I first thought of?

———————————————————

27 I think of a number and divide it by 4. The result is 9 less than the number I first thought of. Find the number I first thought of.

———————————————————

28 The perimeter of a rectangle is 24 cm. It is twice as long as it is wide. How long is it?

———————————————————

29 Tom is seven times as old as his daughter Rose. If the difference in their ages is 30 years, how old are Tom and Rose?

———————————————————

30 A man is 25 years older than his son. The sum of their ages is 49 years. How old is the man and the son?

———————————————————

31 A schoolteacher had eight weeks' holiday. He spent part at home, three times as long on a cricket tour and four times as long with his family at a property near the sea. How long did he spend at home?

———————————————————

32 The sum of two numbers is 21 and their difference is 5. Find the two numbers.

———————————————————

33 The sum of three consecutive numbers is 27. Find the numbers.

———————————————————

34 The sum of three consecutive even numbers is 48. Find the numbers.

———————————————————

35 A fishing rod consisting of three pieces, is 450 cm long. Measuring from one end the first piece is x cm long, the second piece is 15 cm longer than the first piece, and the third piece is 15 cm longer than the second piece. Form an equation in x and solve it to find:

a the length of the shortest piece

_____

b the length of the other two pieces.

_____

36 For a concert at the village hall, the Amberley Operatic Society sold 70 tickets at $\$x$ each and 148 tickets at $\$2x$. If the total receipts were $\$5490$ form an equation in x and solve it to find the price of each ticket.

_____

37 Solve the equations:

a $x + 15 = 4x + 3$ _____

b $2(3x - 3) = 9$ _____

38 Simplify:

a $3(1 - 2x) + 9x - 2$ _____

b $4(3x - 5) - 2(3 - 4x)$ _____

39 Write a formula for the perimeter of each of the following shapes.

a

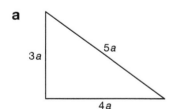

_____

b

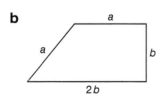

_____

c

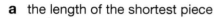

_____

40 If $a = b + c$ find:

a a when $b = 5$ and $c = 10$ _____

b b when $a = 12$ and $c = 3$ _____

41 If $a = 2$, $b = 3$ and $c = 5$ find the value of:

a $a + b$ _____

b $a + 2b$ _____

c $a + b + c$ _____

d $c - a - b$ _____

e $3a - 2b$ _____

f $a + 2b + 3c$ _____

42 If $a = 2$, $b = 4$ and $c = 7$ find the value of:

a $b + c - 3a$ _____

b $10a + 2c$ _____

c $4a - 2b + c$ _____

d $2c - a - 3b$ _____

e $3a - 2b + 2c$ _____

f $3a + 2b - c$ _____

43 If $s = \frac{1}{2}(a + b + c)$ find s when:

a $a = 3$, $b = 5$ and $c = 4$ _____

b $a = 2.5$, $b = 1.7$ and $c = 3.2$ _____

44 Given that $C = 90 - \frac{1}{2}A$, find C when A is:

a 60 _____

b 90 _____

c 0 _____

45 Given that $P = 2(3Q - R)$, find P when $Q = 3$ and $R = -4$.

_____

46 If $a = b + c$ find a when $b = -5$ and $c = -3$.

_____

47 If $v = u + at$, find u when $v = 64$, $a = -5$ and $t = 2$.

_____

48 If $x = wy + 3z$ find:

a x when $w = 5$, $y = 2$ and $z = 3$

_____

b x when $w = 4$, $y = -3$ and $z = 5$

_____

c x when $w = 9$, $y = \frac{1}{2}$ and $z = \frac{1}{3}$

_____

49 A rectangular box is a cm long, b cm wide and c cm deep. If the volume of the box is V cm³, write down a formula for V in terms of the other letters. Use your formula to find:

a V when $a = 12$, $b = 8$ and $c = 6$

_____

b b when $V = 300$, $a = 10$ and $c = 5$

_____

50 Simplify:

a $7a + 4 - 3a - 6 - a + 2$

_____

b $5(a - 3) + 4(2a - 3) - 3(4 - 3a)$

_____

51 Which of the following are expressions and which are equations?

a $3x - 4 = 9$ _____

b $5(2x - 3)$ _____

c $P = 3qr$ _____

d $4(3x - 4) = 12x - 16$ _____

e $3(5x - 7) = x + 2$ _____

f $V = abc$ _____

52 An open rectangular box is a cm long, b cm wide and c cm deep.

Write down an expression for:

a the area of the base of the box

_____

b the total external area of the four sides of the box

_____

c the capacity, or volume, of the box.

_____

4 Inequalities

Form an inequality from the following statements.

For each question choose a letter to represent the variable and state what your letter stands for.

1 There is space for fewer than 10 cars in the school car park.

_____

2 Sara owns at least eight dogs.

_____

3 It takes at least 200 hours to make a violin.

_____

4 Fewer than 200 people attended the concert.

_____

5 The perimeter of a square courtyard is less than 100 m.

_____

6 More than 1000 books were sold on publication day.

_____

7 There are more than 150 ancient trees in our park.

_____

8 There are at least 25 drawers in Peter's study.

_____

9 Use a number line to illustrate the range of values of x for which each of the following inequalities is true:

a $x > 5$

b $x < -5$

c $x > -3$

d $x < 1$

10 Which of the inequalities given in question **9** are satisfied by a value of x equal to:

a 2   _____

b −4   _____

c 0   _____

d 0.3   _____

e −1.7   _____

11 Solve the following inequalities and illustrate your solution on a number line:

a $x - 3 > 5$

17

b $x - 7 < 2$

d $4 - x < -8$

c $x + 3 < 0$

e $7 > x - 4$

d $x + 8 < 4$

13 Use a number line to illustrate the range of values of x for which each of the following inequalities are true:

a $x > 9$

12 Solve the following inequalities and illustrate your solution on a number line:

a $6 < x + 6$

b $x < 5$

b $2 - x > 1$

c $x > -10$

c $8 > 2 - x$

d $x > 1\frac{1}{2}$

e $x < 2.8$

c $5x + 1 > 3$

f $x > -2$

d $4 + 3x < 7$

14 State which of the inequalities given in question **13** are satisfied by a value of:

a 3 _____

b -2 _____

c 2.3 _____

d 0.04 _____

15 For each inequality in question **13**, give a number that satisfies the inequality that is:

a a whole number _____

b not a whole number. _____

16 Solve the following inequalities and illustrate your solution on a number line:

a $4x - 3 > 9$

b $3x - 5 < 4$

17 Solve the following inequalities and illustrate your solution on a number line:

a $2 + 5x \leqslant 7$

b $2x + 3 < x + 2$

c $5 - 3x \leqslant 9$

d $5x - 2 < x + 7$

e $10 \leqslant 3 - 5x$

f $4 - x > -7$

18 Solve the following inequalities and illustrate each inequality on a number line:

a $5 + x > 10$

g $6 - x < -7$

In questions **19** to **23**, solve the inequality and give two integer values of x that satisfy each one.

b $5 < x + 7$

19 a $x - 7 > 8$ _____

b $x - 4 > 9$ _____

c $x - 3 > 1$ _____

20 a $x - 2 < 4$ _____

b $x - 5 < 6$ _____

c $3 > x - 4$

c $x + 2 > 4$ _____

21 a $x + 6 > 9$ _____

b $x + 3 > 10$ _____

c $x + 4 < 8$ _____

d $7 < 5 - x$

22 a $x + 5 < 11$ _____

b $3x - 1 > 8$ _____

c $4x + 7 > 23$ _____

e $2 < -x$

23 a $3x - 5 < 13$ _____

b $5x - 9 < 11$ _____

c $7x - 9 < 12$ _____

24 Consider the true inequality $12 > -6$.
In each case state whether or not the inequality remains true.

a multiply each side by 3

_____

b divide each side by -3

_____

c multiply each side by 0.6

_____

d divide each side by 6

_____

e multiply each side by -2

_____

f divide each side by 3

_____

25 Repeat the previous question with the true inequality $-24 < 12$.

a _____

b _____

c _____

d _____

e _____

f _____

26 Find, where possible, the range of values of x for which the two inequalities are both true:

a $x > 4$ and $x > 6$ _____

b $x \leqslant 4$ and $x \leqslant 6$ _____

c $x < 4$ and $x > 6$ _____

27 Find, where possible, the range of values of x for which the two inequalities are both true:

a $x > 3$ and $x > -1$ _____

b $x \leqslant 3$ and $x > 6$ _____

c $x > -4$ and $x \leqslant 6$ _____

28 Find, where possible, the range of values of x for which the two inequalities are both true:

a $x > 4$, $x > 1$ _____

b $x < 4$, $x \leqslant 1$ _____

c $x < 4$, $x > -1$ _____

d $x \geqslant 4$, $x > -1$ _____

29 Find, where possible, the range of values of x for which the two inequalities are both true:

a $x \geqslant 2$, $x > 0$ _____

b $x \geqslant -2$, $x > 0$ _____

c $x \leqslant 2$, $x < 0$ _____

d $x \leqslant -2$, $x < 0$ _____

In questions **30** to **35**, solve each pair of inequalities. Then find the range of values of x which satisfies both inequalities.

30 $4 - x > 2$ and $3 + x > 1$

_____

31 $x - 3 \leqslant 4$ and $x + 5 \geqslant 4$

_____

32 $3 - 2x \leqslant 5$ and $1 + 4x < 9$

_____

33 $0 > 1 - 3x$ and $2x - 7 \leqslant 1$

_____

34 $2x + 3 > 5$ and $3x - 2 < 4$

_____

35 $x - 5 \leqslant 2$ and $x + 7 \geqslant 5$

_____

36 Solve each pair of inequalities and then find the range of values of x which satisfy both of them:

a $x - 3 < 7, x + 2 > 1$ _____

b $2x - 3 > 3, 3x - 7 < 14$ _____

c $3x - 2 > 8, 3x - 2 \leqslant x + 4$ _____

d $5x \leqslant 4x - 3, 3x < x + 8$ _____

e $x + 4 < 8, x - 2 > 3$ _____

37 Solve each of the following pairs of inequalities and then find the range of values of x that satisfy both of them:

a $3x - 3 < 4x + 1 < 9$ _____

b $2x + 5 > x - 3 > 2$ _____

c $3 - x < 2x + 3 < 5$ _____

d $3 - 4x < 2x - 2 < 1$ _____

e $4 - 3x < 2x + 1 < 6$ _____

38 a Solve the inequalities and illustrate each solution on a number line.

  i $5 > 7 + x$

  ii $3x - 1 > 5$

b Solve the inequalities

  i $x - 3 < 7$ and $x + 2 > 4$

  _____

ii Now find the range of values of x which satisfies both inequalities.

_____

39 Solve the following inequalities and illustrate each solution on a number line:

a $3 \geqslant 8 - 5x$

b $7 - 4x \geqslant 3$

c $2x + 2 > 6 - x$

d $2 - x > 2x - 1$

e $2x - 5 > x - 3$

f $4x + 2 > 5x + 2$

46 $\{x \mid x \geqslant -2\}$

Write these inequalities in set builder notation.

47 $\{x \mid -3 < x \leqslant 4\}$

40 $x > 10$

_____

41 $3 < x < 8$

_____ **48** $\{x \mid 2 < x < 5\}$

42 $4 < x < 7$

_____

43 $-5 \leqslant x \leqslant 0$

_____ **49** $\{x \mid x \geqslant -5.5\}$

Illustrate these inequalities on a number line.

44 $\{x \mid x > 4\}$

50 $\{x \mid -2 \leqslant x < 6\}$

45 $\{x \mid 3 < x \leqslant 6\}$

5 Sets

1 Write down, in words, the given set:

   a {2, 4, 6, 8} _____

   b {2, 3, 5, 7} _____

2 Describe a set that includes the given members of the following sets and state another member of each one.

   a {20, 25, 30, 35, 40}

   _____

   b {Oregon, California, Nebraska, Texas}

   _____

   c {saucepan, kettle, colander, chopping board}

   _____

3 Describe a universal set that includes the given members of the following sets. Then state another member in the universal set.

   a {18, 24, 30, 36}

   _____

   b {Martinique, St Lucia, St Vincent, Grenada}

   _____

   c {hammer, pincers, saw, brace}

   _____

4 Write each of the following in set notation:

   a Caryl is a member of the set of boys' names.

   _____

   b A parrot is not a tree.

   _____

   c A carpet is a type of floor covering.

   _____

d 11 is a prime number.

   _____

5 Write each of the following statements in set notation:

   a James is a member of the set of boys' names.

   _____

   b A triangle is a mathematical shape.

   _____

   c A bus is not a mountain.

   _____

6 State whether the following statements are true or false:

   a $31 \in$ {prime numbers} _____

   b Rome $\in$ {European countries}

   _____

   c rhombus $\in$ {quadrilaterals}

   _____

7 How many elements are there in each of these sets?

   a {even numbers less than 20}

   _____

   b {odd numbers between 8 and 20}

   _____

   c {prime numbers between 25 and 40}

   _____

   d {multiples of 4 between 1 and 25}

   _____

8 How many elements are there in each of these sets?

a {days of the week}

_____

b {months of the year}

_____

c {prime numbers between 20 and 30}

_____

9 Are the following sets finite or infinite?

a {the number of people in the world}

_____

b {the decimal numbers between 1 and 2}

_____

c {the positive integers bigger than 100}

_____

10 If $n(A)$ is the number of elements in set A, find $n(A)$ for each of the following sets:

a A = {different letters in the word PARALLELOGRAM}

_____

b A = {players in a hockey team}

_____

c A = {letters in the alphabet}

_____

d A = {states in the USA}

_____

11 If $n(A)$ is the number of elements in set A, find $n(A)$ for each of the following sets:

a A = {different letters in the word MATHEMATICS}

_____

b A = {players in a cricket team}

_____

c A = {different letters in the word CARIBBEAN}

_____

12 Determine whether or not the following sets are null sets:

a {men that have walked on the moon}

_____

b {multiples of 9 between 10 and 20}

_____

c {dogs with six legs}

_____

13 U = {whole numbers from 10 to 40 inclusive}
P = {multiples of 4}
Q = {multiples of 5}

In each case describe, in words, the set represented by the shaded area.

a

b

c

d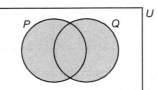

_____

e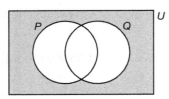

_____

14 If Q = {integers from 10 to 40} list the following subsets:

R = {multiples of 3 and 4}

_____

S = {prime numbers}

_____

T = {odd numbers that are not prime numbers}

_____

15 Suggest a universal set for:

a {8, 16, 24, 32, 40}

_____

b {car, bus, lorry, motorcycle}

_____

16 U = {integers from 20 to 40 inclusive}

A = {prime numbers}

B = {multiples of 6}

Find:

a n(A) _____

b n(B) _____

17 If A = {odd numbers from 4 to 24}, list the following subsets of A:

B = {multiples of 4}

_____

C = {prime numbers}

_____

D = {odd numbers greater than 15}

_____

18 If P = {integers from 1 to 30}, list the following subsets of P:

Q = {prime numbers}

_____

R = {multiples of both 2 and 3}

_____

S = {even prime numbers}

_____

19 U = {whole numbers from 1 to 20 inclusive}

A = {multiples of 3}

B = {multiples of 4}

In each case describe, in words, the set represented by the shaded area.

a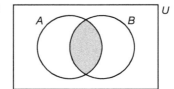

_____

b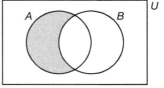

_____

c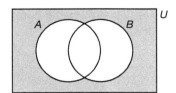

---

20 U = {letters of the alphabet}

P = {letters in the word ARITHMETIC}

Q = {letters in the word MATHEMATICS}

a Find the union of P and Q, illustrating your answer on a Venn diagram.

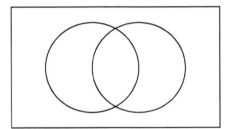

b Find:

i $n(P)$ = _____

ii $n(Q)$ = _____

21 U = {letters of the alphabet}

X = {letters in the word AMERICA}

Y = {letters in the word BRITAIN}

a Find the union of X and Y, illustrating your answer as a Venn diagram.

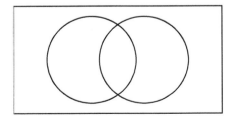

b Find:

i $n(X)$ = _____

ii $n(Y)$ = _____

In questions **22** and **23**, show on a Venn diagram the intersections of the given sets. In each case write down the intersection in set notation.

22 U = {integers from 5 to 15 inclusive}

P = {7, 11, 13}, Q = {10, 11, 14, 15}

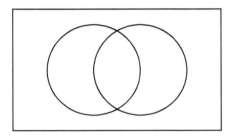

---

23 U = {positive whole numbers}

X = {odd numbers that divide exactly into 36}

Y = {odd numbers that divide exactly into 24}

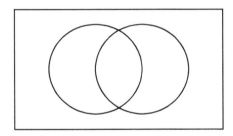

---

24 Suggest a universal set for the members of the sets given in this Venn diagram.

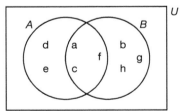

U = _____

Find:

a $n(A)$ _____

b $n(B)$ _____

c $n(A \cup B)$ _____

d $n(A \cap B)$ _____

25 Set P has five members and set Q has seven members.

a What is the largest possible number of members for the set $P \cup Q$?

_____

b What is the largest possible number of members for the set $P \cap Q$?

_____

c What is the smallest possible number of members for the set $P \cup Q$?

_____

d What is the smallest possible number of members for the set $P \cap Q$?

_____

26 Set A has 4 members and set B has 10 members.

a What is the largest possible number of members for set $A \cup B$?

_____

b What is the largest possible number of members for set $A \cap B$?

_____

c What is the smallest possible number of members for set $A \cup B$?

_____

d What is the smallest possible number of members for set $A \cap B$?

_____

27 Set P has six members and set Q has five members.

a What is the largest possible number of members for set $P \cup Q$?

_____

b What is the largest possible number of members for set $P \cap Q$?

_____

c What is the smallest possible number of members for set $P \cup Q$?

_____

d What is the smallest possible number of members for set $P \cap Q$?

_____

28 $U = \{$letters of the alphabet$\}$

$C = \{$letters used in the word TRINIDAD$\}$

$D = \{$letters used in the word DOMINICA$\}$

Find:

a $n(U)$, $n(C)$ and $n(D)$

_____

b Show these as a Venn diagram

c Hence find:

i $C \cap D$ **ii** $C \cup D$

d Describe each set in part **c**.

i _____

ii _____

29 $U = \{$whole numbers less than 10$\}$

$X = \{$prime numbers less than 10$\}$

$Y = \{$odd numbers less than 10$\}$

a Find $n(U)$, $n(X)$ and $n(Y)$

_____

b Find $n(X \cap Y)$ and $n(X \cup Y)$

_____

30 U = {my friends}

A = {my friends who play tennis}

B = {my friends who swim}

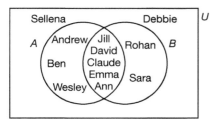

List everyone who:

a play tennis

_____

_____

b swim but do not play tennis

_____

_____

c play tennis and swim

_____

_____

d neither swim nor play tennis.

_____

_____

31 U = {whole numbers from 4 to 34 inclusive}

K = {multiples of 6 between 4 and 34}

L = {multiples of 5 between 4 and 34}

Illustrate this information as a Venn diagram

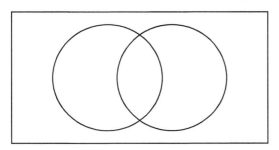

Hence find:

a $n(K)$ _____

b $n(L)$ _____

c $n(K \cup L)$ _____

d $n(K \cap L)$ _____

32 U = {letters of the alphabet}

P = {letters used in the word ARITHMETIC}

Q = {letters used in the word CARIBBEAN}

a Find:

i $n(U)$ _____

ii $n(P)$ _____

iii $n(Q)$ _____

b Show these on a Venn diagram.

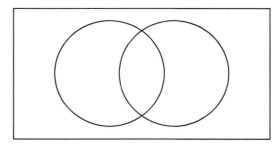

33 If N = {the positive integers 1 to 12 inclusive}, list the following subsets of N:

a A = {even numbers from 1 to 12 inclusive}

_____

b B = {prime numbers <12}

_____

c C = {multiples of 3 that are less than or equal to 12}

_____

d Do sets A and B have any element in common?

_____

34 U = (whole numbers from 15 to 29 inclusive}

A = {even numbers between 15 and 29}

B = {multiples of 3 between 16 and 29}

Illustrate this information on a Venn diagram.

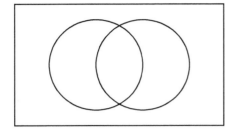

Write:

a the even numbers between 15 and 30 that are multiples of 3

_____

b $n(A)$ and $n(B)$.

_____

35 U = {pupils in a class}

A = {pupils who like science}

B = {pupils who like maths}

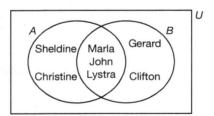

List the set of pupils who:

a like maths but not science

_____

b like both subjects

_____

c like science but not maths.

_____

36 U = {whole numbers from 3 to 30 inclusive}

P = {multiples of 4 between 3 and 30 inclusive}

Q = {multiples of 5 between 3 and 30 inclusive}

Illustrate this information on a Venn diagram.

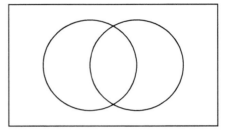

Write:

a the numbers between 3 and 30 that are multiples of both 4 and 5

_____

b $n(P)$ _____

c $n(Q)$ _____

d $n(P \cup Q)$ _____

37 U = {letters of the alphabet}

X = {letters in the word CARIBBEAN}

Y = {letters in the word ISLANDS}

Illustrate this information on a Venn diagram.

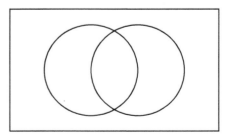

Write:

a $n(X)$ _____

b $n(Y)$ _____

c $n(X \cup Y)$ _____

d $n(X \cap Y)$ _____

38 U = {my friends}

A = {friends who wear wristwatches}

B = {friends who walk to school}

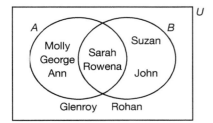

a List all my friends who:

   i wear wristwatches

   _____

   ii walk to school

   _____

b Find:

   i $n(A \cup B)$

   _____

   ii $n(A \cap B)$

   _____

39 U = {boys in my class}

X = {boys who are good at maths}

  = {Neil, Monty, Arthur, Colville, Myrick, Bill}

Y = {boys who play cricket}

  = {Derek, Neil, Myrick, Norman, Lloyd}

Illustrate this information on a Venn diagram.

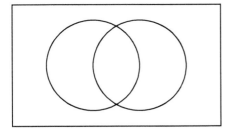

Use this diagram to write down the following sets:

a {boys who are good at maths and play cricket}

_____

b {boys who play cricket but are not good at maths}

_____

c If $n(U) = 25$ find the number of boys who are neither good at maths nor play cricket.

40 A and B are two sets where $n(A \cap B) = 2$ and $n(U) = 30$

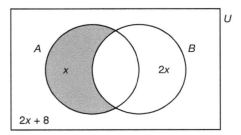

a Form an equation in x and solve it.

_____

b Find $n(A \cup B)$ and $n(A \cup B)'$.

_____

6 Relations

1 Describe the relation between the second and the first number in each pair in this set:

{(1, 5), (2, 10), (3, 15), (4, 20)}

_____

2 Describe the relation between the second and the first number in each pair in this set:

{(1, 4), (3, 6), (5, 8), (7, 10)}

_____

3 This table shows the name and number of CDs owned by three pupils.

Name	Number of CDs
Sally	20
Don	13
Victor	34

Write the set of ordered pairs in the relation described as, 'The second pupil in each pair has more CDs than the first.'

_____

4 The second number in each pair in this relation is the square of the first number. Fill in the missing numbers.

{(3, 9), (6,   ), (, 100)}

5 The second number in each pair in this relation is the next prime number that is larger than the first number. Fill in the missing numbers.

{(6, 7), (8,   ), (15,   ), (21,   )}

6 The first number in each pair is half the second number. Fill in the missing numbers.

(, 12), (, 18), (4,   )

7 The second number in each pair is the reciprocal of the first number. Fill in the missing numbers.

$(2,   ), (, 5), \left(\frac{1}{4},   \right)$

8 The second letter in each pair is the next letter in the alphabet after the first letter. Fill in the missing letters.

(p,   ), (b,   ), (n,   )

9 Write the domain and range of the relation {(1, 4), (3, 6), (5, 8), (7, 10)}

_____

10 Write the domain and range of the relation {(1, 8), (3, 10), (5, 12), (7, 14)}

_____

11 The set {3, 5, 7} is the domain of a relation. The second number in each ordered pair is the square of the first. What is the range?

_____

12 Henderson, Stuart and Anthony are three boys. Stuart is heavier than Henderson and Anthony is heavier than Stuart.

a Write the relation described as 'first boy in each pair is heavier than the second boy'.

_____

b Give the domain. _____

c Give the range. _____

13 Write the domain and range of each relation.

a {(p, q), (p, r), (p, s), (r, t)}

Domain _____

Range _____

b {(1, 4), (2, 7), (3, 10), (4, 13)}

Domain _____

Range _____

14 April lives 2 km from school, Jason lives 500 m from school and Cherie lives 1.5 km from school.

   a Write the relationship described as 'the first child in each pair lives nearer to school than the second child'.

   _____

   b Give the domain. _____

   c Give the range. _____

15 The letters in the word MATHS form the basis of a relation.

   a Write the relationship described as 'the first letter in each pair is later in the alphabet than the second letter'.

   _____

   b Give the range. _____

16 Each diagram represents a relation. Write the relation as a set of ordered pairs.

   a

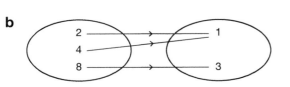

   _____

   b

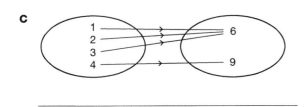

   _____

   c

   _____

17 Each diagram represents a relation. Write the relation as a set of ordered pairs.

   a

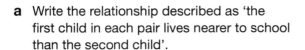

   _____

   b

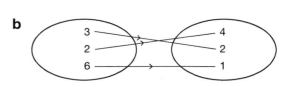

   _____

   c

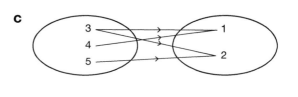

   _____

18 Write the type of relationship shown in each part of question **16**.

   a _____

   b _____

   c _____

19 Write the type of relationship shown in each part of question **17**.

   a _____

   b _____

   c _____

20 Represent each relation as a table of values where x is the first number in the pair.

a {(1, 3), (2, 5), (3, 7), (4, 9)}

x	1	2	3	4
y				

b {(3, 1), (6, 2), (9, 3), (12, 4)}

x				
y				

c {(12, 9), (10, 7), (9, 6), (5, 2)}

x				
y				

21 Draw a mapping diagram to represent each mapping given in question **20**.

a

b

c

22 Write the type of each relation given in question **20**.

a _____

b _____

c _____

23 A relation is represented by this table.

x	4	6	10
y	2	3	5

What type of relation is this?

_____

24 A relation is represented by this table.

x	–2	2	3	4
y	4	4	9	16

a Draw a mapping diagram to represent this relation.

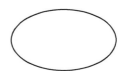 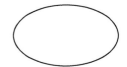

b What type of relation is this?

_____

25 A relation is represented by this table.

x	1	1	2	4
y	2	3	3	15

a Draw a mapping diagram to represent this relation.

 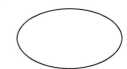

b What type of relation is this?

_____

26 A relation is given by {(x, y)} where $y = 4x$ for $x = 1, 2, 3$

a Complete this table of values.

x	1	2	3
y		8	

b Write the domain.

_____

c Write the range.

_____

27 A relation is given by $\{(x, y)\}$ where
$y = 15 - 3x$ for $x = 1, 2, 3$ and 5

  a Complete this table of values.

x	1	2	3	5
y		9		

  b Write the domain.

  _____

  c Write the range.

  _____

28 A relation is given by $\{(x, y)\}$ where
$y = 3 + x^2$ for $x = 1, 2, 3, 4$

  a Complete this table of values.

x	1	2	3	4
y			12	

  b Write the domain.

  _____

  c Write the range.

  _____

29 A relation is given by $\{(x, y)\}$ where
$y = x^2 + 3x - 4$ for $x = 1, 2, 3, 4$

  a Complete this table of values.

x	1	2	3	4
y			14	

  b Write the domain.

  _____

  c Write the range.

  _____

30 A relation is given by $\{(x, y)\}$ where
$y = 2x^2 - x$ for $x = 1, 2, 3, 4$

  a Complete this table of values.

x	1	2	3	4
y		6		

  b Write the domain.

  _____

  c Write the range.

  _____

31 A relation is given by $\{(x, y)\}$ where
$y = x^3 - x^2 + 4$ for $x = 0, 1, 2, 3$

  a Complete this table of values.

x	0	1	2	3
y			8	

  b Write the domain.

  _____

  c Write the range.

  _____

  d What type of relation is this?

  _____

Review test 1: units 1 to 6

In questions **1** to **12**, choose the letter that gives the correct answer.

1 $12 - 3(9 - 5) =$

  A 24   **B** 12

  C 6   **D** 0

2 Which law, if any, does the following statement illustrate?

  $5 \times (3 - 1) = 5 \times 3 + 5 \times (-1)$

  A commutative   **B** associative

  C distributive   **D** none of these

3 The inverse of 3 under addition is:

  A -3 **B** $-\dfrac{1}{3}$

  C $\dfrac{1}{3}$ **D** 3

4 The value of 4.9273 correct to 2 s.f. is:

  A 4.9   **B** 4.92

  C 4.93   **D** 5.0

5 64% as a fraction in its lowest terms is:

  A $\dfrac{64}{100}$ **B** $\dfrac{32}{50}$

  C $\dfrac{16}{25}$ **D** none of these

6 The value of 0.005 473 correct to 3 s.f. is:

  A 0.005 47   **B** 0.0055

  C 0.005   **D** 0.010

7 $\dfrac{3}{8}$ written as a decimal is:

  A 0.3   **B** 0.375

  C 0.8   **D** 0.875

8 $0.1 \div 0.001 =$

  A 10   **B** 100

  C 1000   **D** 10000

9 As a single expression, the value of $2^3 \times 2^4$ is:

  A 2^1 **B** 2^7

  C 2^9 **D** 2^{12}

10 The value of $(-8 - (-3)) \times (+5)$ is:

  A -25 **B** -23

  C 7   **D** 25

11 If X is the point $(3, -2)$, the coordinates of the point 3 to the left and 4 above is:

  A $(6, -6)$ **B** $(6, -2)$

  C $(6, 2)$ **D** $(0, 2)$

12 45% as a fraction in its lowest terms is:

  A $\dfrac{45}{100}$ **B** $\dfrac{27}{60}$

  C $\dfrac{9}{20}$ **D** 0.45

13 Give:

  a 43 542 correct to 1 s.f. _____

  b 4 260 000 correct to 2 s.f. _____

14 Change 55% into:

  a a fraction in its lowest term _____

  b a decimal.   _____

15 A book contains four short stories. The first is $\frac{1}{6}$ of the whole, the second is $\frac{1}{8}$ of the whole, the third has 126 pages, and the fourth is $\frac{1}{3}$ of the whole. How many pages are there in the book?

_____

16 $5 - 2(3x - 2)$ simplifies to:

  A $1 - 6x$ **B** $9 - 5x$

  C $7 - 6x$ **D** $9 - 6x$

17 $3(2 - x) + 3(3 - x)$ simplifies to:

    A 15   **B** -15

    C $15 - 6x$ **D** $6x - 15$

18 The solution of the equation $25 - 4x = 4 + 3x$ is:

    A 2   **B** 3

    C 4   **D** 5

19 Given that $x = 2y - 3z$, if $y = -4$ and $z = -3$ then $x =$

    A -1 **B** 1

    C 12   **D** 17

20 The value of $-8 - 3 - (-12)$ is:

    A -23 **B** -17

    C 1   **D** 7

21 I think of a number and increase its value by $\frac{1}{3}$. Half of the answer is 8. The number I first thought of was:

    A 6   **B** 8

    C 12   **D** 16

22 Write:

    a 27_{10} in base 5   _____

    b 34_5 in base 10   _____

23 Find:

    a $12_4 + 231_4$ _____

    b $31_5 - 14_5$ _____

    c $23_5 \times 3_5$ _____

    d $321_4 \times 2_4$ _____

24 Write:

    a 310_5 to the base 10   _____

    b 24_{10} to the base 5   _____

    c 46_8 to the base 10   _____

    d 11011_2 to the base 10 _____

25 Find:

    a $21_3 + 2_3$ _____

    b $1010_2 + 1011_2$ _____

    c $305_6 - 143_6$ _____

    d $33_4 - 22_4$ _____

26 Write the denary number 25 as a number to the base:

    a 8 _____

    b 5 _____

    c 3 _____

27 A rectangle is a cm long and b cm wide.

    a Write a formula for P, where P cm is its perimeter.

    b Write a formula for A, where A cm^2 is its area.

28 A packet of tea has a mass of m g. An empty carton has a mass of n g. When the carton is packed with 24 packets of tea it has a mass of Q g. Write a formula for Q.

_____

29 If $D = 5(2e - f)$ find D when $e = -12$ and $f = 16$.

_____

30 If $A = \dfrac{PRT}{100}$ find A when $P = 200$, $R = 3$ and $T = 4$.

_____

31 Given that $P = q \div r$ find q when $P = 20$ and $r = 7$.

_____

32 Write 796 382 correct to:

    a 2 s.f.   _____

    b 3 s.f.   _____

    c the nearest hundred   _____

    d the nearest thousand. _____

In questions **33** to **38**, solve the given inequalities

33 a $x - 6 > 8$ _____

 b $x - 4 > 9$ _____

 c $x - 3 > 2$ _____

34 a $x - 2 < 4$ _____

 b $x - 5 < 7$ _____

 c $x + 2 > 4$ _____

35 a $x + 6 > 9$ _____

 b $x + 3 > 10$ _____

 c $x + 4 < 8$ _____

36 a $x + 5 < 12$ _____

 b $3x - 1 > 8$ _____

 c $4x + 7 > 23$ _____

37 a $3x - 5 < 10$ _____

 b $5x - 7 < 8$ _____

 c $7x - 3 > 11$ _____

38 a $4x + 5 < 6x + 1$ _____

 b $3x - 7 > 4x - 2$ _____

In questions **39** to **43**, solve each of the pairs of inequalities. Then find the range of values of x which satisfies both of them.

39 $x - 3 < 7$ and $x + 1 > 3$

_____

40 $5 - x > 2$ and $3 + x > 3$

_____

41 $2x - 1 > 5$ and $3x - 2 < 13$

_____

42 $2x + 3 > 4$ and $3x - 5 \leqslant 2$

_____

43 $2x - 5 > 9$ and $\frac{1}{2}x + 2 < 5$

_____

44 Illustrate the following inequalities on a number line:

 a $\{x \mid x > 3\}$

 b $\{x \mid x \leqslant -2\}$

 c $\{x \mid 0 \leqslant x < 4\}$

 d $\{x \mid -3 < x \leqslant -2\}$

45

 a Describe in words:

  i the universal set

  _____

  ii set A

  _____

  iii set B.

  _____

 b Find:

  i $n(A \cup B)$ _____

  ii $n(A \cap B)$ _____

46 U = {letters in the alphabet}

P = {different letters in the word FAMILY}

Q = {different letters in the word HISTORY}

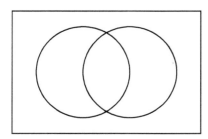

Show these letters on the Venn diagram and hence write:

a $n(P)$ _____

b $n(Q)$ _____

c $n(P \cup Q)$ _____

d $n(P \cap Q)$ _____

47 What type of relation is {(0,0), (1,5), (2,6),(3,5), (4,6)}

A $1 : 1$ **B** $1 : n$

C $n : 1$ **D** $n : n$

48 a Write the domain and range of {(1,4), (2,5), (4,7), (10,13)}

_____

b Draw a mapping diagram to represent the relation {(2,5), (3,10), (4,17), (5,26)}

c What type of relation does this diagram represent?

_____

49 A relation is given by {(x,y)} where $y = 5 + 2x$ for $x = 2, 4, 6, 8$

Copy and complete this table of values:

x	2	4	6	8
y		13		

50 A relation is given by {(x,y)} where $y = x^2$ for $x = -2, -1, 0, 1, 2, 3$

a Copy and complete this table of values:

x	−2	−1	0	1	2	3
y		1				

b Write the domain and range.

_____

c Represent the relation with a mapping diagram.

d What type of relation is this?

_____

1 Write the coordinates of the points

A(,   ), B(,   ),

C(,   ), D(,   ),

E(,   ), F(,   ),

G(,   ), H(,   ).

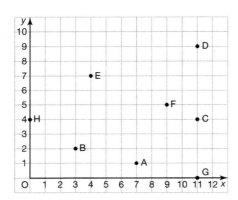

2 Mark the following points on the grid:

A(2, 3), B(10, 6), C(7, 10), D(3, 7), E(14, 2), F(12, 0), G(8, 3), H(8, 1).

Join the points in alphabetical order and join A to H.

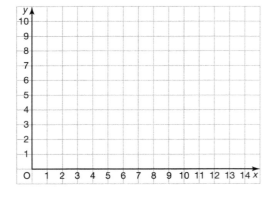

3 Mark the following points on the grid:

A(3, 1), B(3, 5), C(10, 5), D(10, 1).

Join A to B, B to C, C to D and D to A.

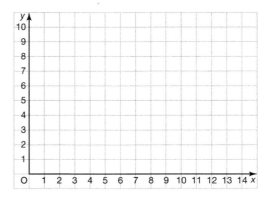

What is the name of the figure ABCD?

_____

4 Mark the following points on the grid:

A(2, 6), B(9, 8), C(11, 4), D(4, 2).

Join A to B, B to C, C to D and D to A.

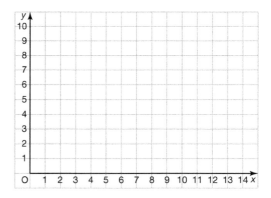

What is the name of the figure ABCD?

_____

5 Mark the following points on the grid:

A(2, 9), B(12, 9), C(10, 3), D(4, 3).

Join A to B, B to C, C to D and D to A.

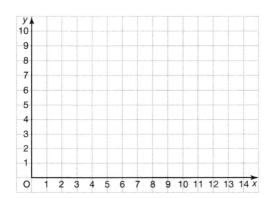

What is the name of the figure ABCD?

_____

6 Mark the points A(2, 6), B(11, 9) and C(14, 0).

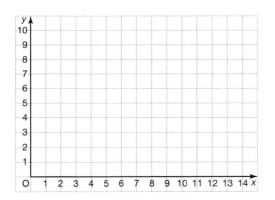

What type of triangle is ABC?

_____

7 The points A(6, 2), B(2, 7) and C(10, 9) are three of the vertices of a parallelogram. Mark the points A, B and C.

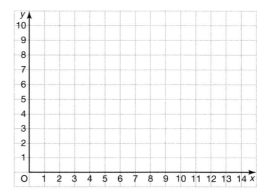

Find the point D and write its coordinates.

_____

8 The points A(2, 2), B(2, 8) and C(12, 2) are the vertices of a triangle ABC. Plot these points and mark D the midpoint of AB, E the midpoint of AC, and F the midpoint of BC.

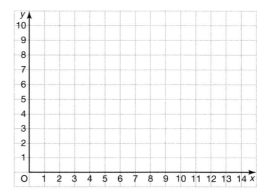

Write the coordinates of:

D _____

E _____

F _____

What is special about triangle ABC?

_____

Does triangle DEF have the same property?

_____

9

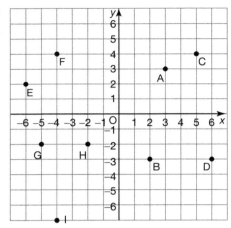

a Write the *x*-coordinate of each of the points A, B, C, D, E, F, G, H and I. O is the origin.

_____

_____

_____

b Write the *y*-coordinate of each of the points A, B, C, D, E, F, G, H and I. O is the origin.

_____

_____

_____

10

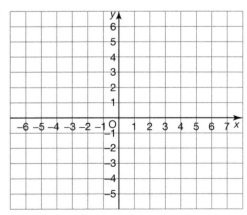

Mark the points A(2, 2), B(6, 4), C(4, 4), D(−4, 5), E(−5, 2), F(−3, −3), G(2, −2) and H(7, 1). Join the points in order and join H to A.

11

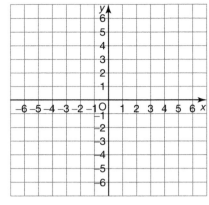

The points A(−4, 4), B(2, 4) and C(2, −2) are three corners of a square ABCD. Mark these points on the axes and plot the point D. Write the coordinates of D.

_____

12 The points A, B, C, D and E are all on the same straight line.

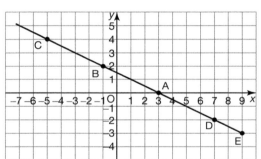

a Write the coordinates of the points A, B, C, D and E.

_____

_____

_____

_____

_____

b How is the *y*-coordinate related to the *x*-coordinate?

_____

_____

_____

c F is another point on this line.
Its *x*-coordinate is –3.
What is its *y*-coordinate?

_____

d G and H are two other points on the line.
Fill in the missing coordinates.

G(, 5), H(5,   ).

13 A, B, C, D, E and F are points on the same straight line.

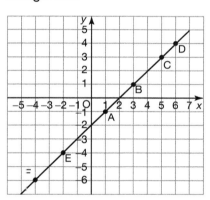

a Write the coordinates of the points A, B, C, D, E and F.

_____

_____

_____

b How is the *y*-coordinate related to the *x*-coordinate?

_____

_____

c G is another point on this line.
Its *x*-coordinate is –3.
What is its *y*-coordinate?

_____

d H and I are two other points on the line.
Fill in the missing coordinates.

H(, –2), I(4,   ).

14 Mark the points A(–5, 1), B(1, 4), C(7, 1) and D(1, –2) on the graph and join ABCD to form a quadrilateral.

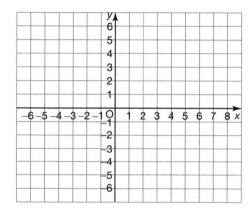

a Join A to C and B to D. These are the diagonals of the quadrilateral. Mark the point where they cross as point E, and write the coordinates of E.

_____

b Measure the diagonals

AC = _____   BD = _____

c Is E the midpoint of either diagonal?

_____

d Do the diagonals cross at right angles?

_____

15 Find the *y*-coordinates of the points on the line $y = -2x$ that have *x*-coordinates:

a 3 _____   **b** $-4\frac{1}{2}$ _____

c 5 _____   **d** –1.3 _____

16 Find the *x*-coordinates of the points on the line $y = \frac{3}{2}x$ that have *y*-coordinates:

a 9 _____   **b** 2 _____

c –3 _____   **d** 1 _____

17 Find the *x*-coordinate of the points on the line $y = -2x$ that have *y*-coordinates:

a 8 _____   **b** 4 _____

c –3 _____   **d** –1 _____

18 Find the *y*-coordinate of the points on the line $y = -\frac{1}{2}x$ that have *x*-coordinates:

a –6 _____   **b** 8 _____

c –1 _____   **d** 3 _____

19 Using 1 cm to 1 unit on each axis plot the points (–3, 9), (–1, 3), (0, 0), (2, –6). What is the equation of the straight line that passes through these points?

_____

20 Which of the points (–2, –4), (–1, 2), (2, –4), (6, 12) lie on the line $y = -2x$?

_____

21 Which of the points (1, –1), (–1, 4), (–1, –5), (2, 2) lie:

a above the line $y = \frac{3}{2}x$? _____

b below the line $y = \frac{3}{2}x$? _____

22 The points (*a*, 5), (6, *b*) and (*c*, –1) lie on the straight line with equation $y = 2x$. Find the values of *a*, *b* and *c*.

a _____   *b* _____   *c* _____

23 The points (–1, *a*), (*b*, 8) and (–8, *c*) lie on the straight line with equation $y = -\frac{1}{4}x$. Find the values of *a*, *b* and *c*.

a _____   *b* _____   *c* _____

24 The equations of four straight lines are:

A $y = -4x$

B $y = 3x$

C $y = \frac{1}{2}x$

D $y = -2x$.

a Which lines have a positive gradient?

_____

b Which lines have a negative gradient?

_____

c Which of the lines with a positive gradient is the steeper?

_____

d Which lines make an acute angle with the positive *x*-axis?

_____

e Which lines make an obtuse angle with the positive *x*-axis?

_____

25 Complete the following table and use it to draw the graph of $y = \frac{3}{4}x$

x	–4	–2	2	4
y				

26 Complete the following table and use it to draw the graph of $y = -\frac{3}{4}x$

x	-4	0	4
y			

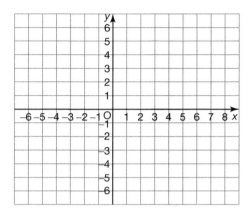

27 For the following equations of straight lines write:

i the gradient m

ii the y-intercept c.

a $y = 5x + 3$ **i** _____   **ii** _____

b $y = 2x - 5$ **i** _____   **ii** _____

c $y = -\frac{1}{2}x + 4$ **i** _____   **ii** _____

d $y = -4x + 7$ **i** _____   **ii** _____

28 Plot the points A(-1, -5), B(0, 0) and C(1, 5), all of which lie on the line $y = 5x$.

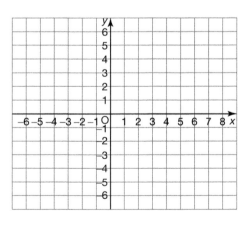

Find the gradient of:

a AB _____

b BC _____

c AC _____

What do you notice?

_____

29 Write the value of:

i the gradient m, and **ii** the y-intercept c, for the straight lines with the following equations:

a $y = 5 - 2x$ **i** $m =$ _____   **ii** $c =$ _____

b $y = 2 - 6x$ **i** $m =$ _____   **ii** $c =$ _____

c $y = 3(x + 2)$ **i** $m =$ _____   **ii** $c =$ _____

d $y = 4(5 - x)$ **i** $m =$ _____   **ii** $c =$ _____

e $y = -2(3x + 1)$ **i** $m =$ _____   **ii** $c =$ _____

f $y = -4(2 - 3x)$ **i** $m =$ _____   **ii** $c =$ _____

30 Write the equations of the straight lines that have the given gradients and y-intercepts:

a gradient 3, y-intercept -3

_____

b gradient $-\frac{3}{2}$, y-intercept 2

_____

c gradient -2, y-intercept 5

_____

d gradient $-\frac{1}{2}$, y-intercept $-\frac{3}{2}$

_____

e gradient $-\frac{1}{3}$, y-intercept -2

_____

31 Draw the lines $y = 3$, $y = -1$ and $y = 5$. Label each line.

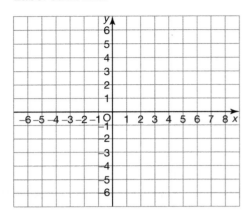

32 Draw the lines $x = 3$, $x = -2$ and $x = -5$. Label each line.

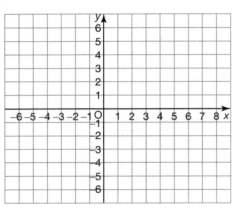

33 Draw the lines $x = -4$, $y = -2$ and $x = 6$. Label each line.

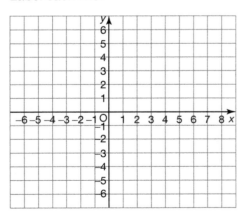

In questions **34** to **37**, write the inequalities that define the unshaded regions.

34

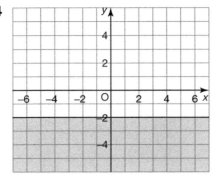

35

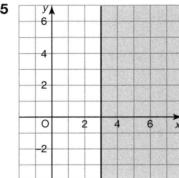

36

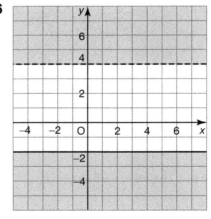

37

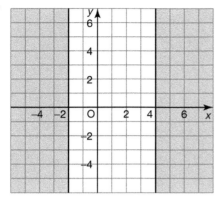

In questions **38** to **44**, give the inequalities that define the shaded regions.

38

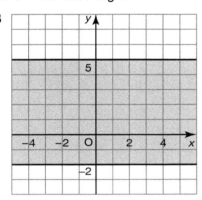

39

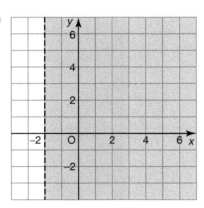

40

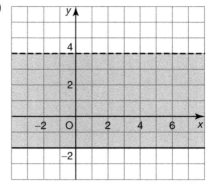

41

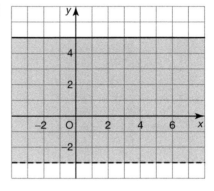

42

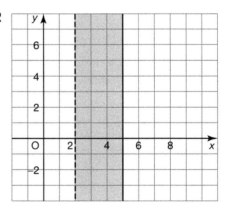

43

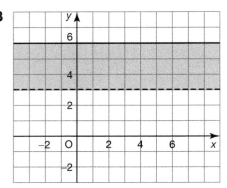

46

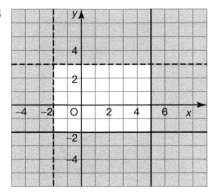

44

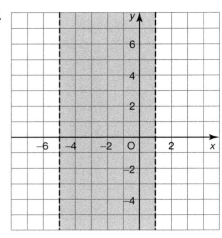

47

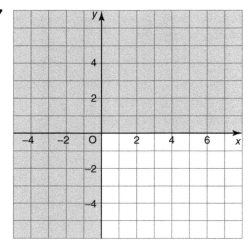

In questions **45** to **49**, write the sets of inequalities that describe the unshaded region.

45

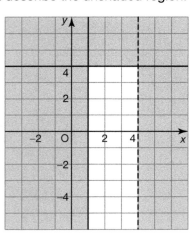

48

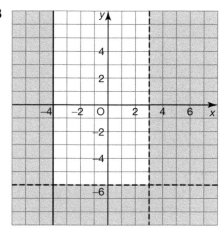

49

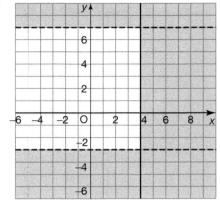

52 $-4 < x \leqslant 3, 2 < y \leqslant 3$

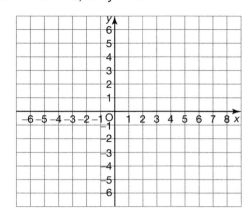

53 $3 < x \leqslant 4, -3 \leqslant y < 2$

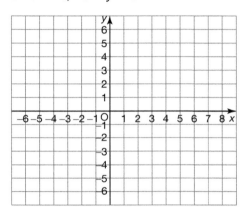

In questions **50** to **53**, represent the regions described by the following inequalities:

50 $2 \leqslant x \leqslant 4, 1 \leqslant y \leqslant 4$

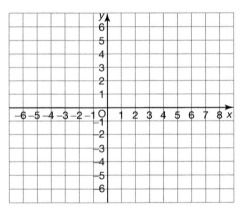

51 $-1 \leqslant x < 3, -2 \leqslant y < 2$

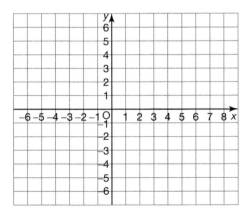

In questions **1** to **4**, complete the drawing so that the broken lines are axes of symmetry.

1
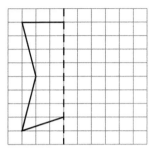

5
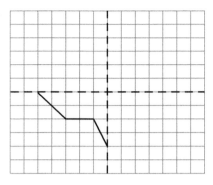

2
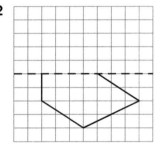

In questions **6** to **10**, draw the reflection of each object in the mirror line.

6
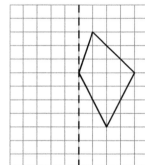

3
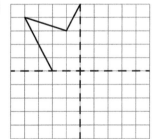

7
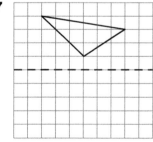

4
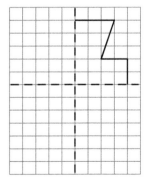

8
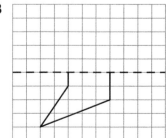

9

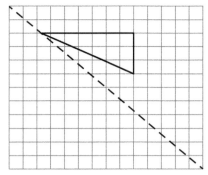

10

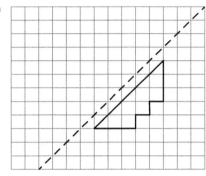

In questions **11** to **15**, draw the reflection of the given object in the mirror line. The vertices of the object are labelled A,B,C, etc. Label the corresponding images of the vertices A′, B′, C′, etc.

11

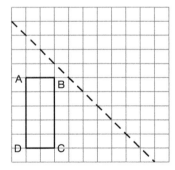

12

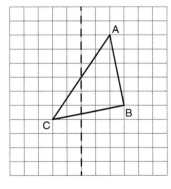

13

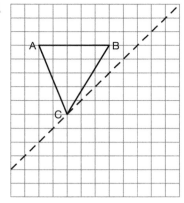

14

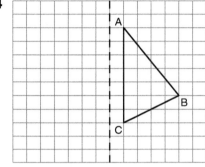

15

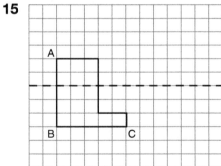

In questions **16** to **18**, draw the mirror line.

16

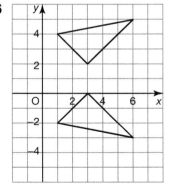

17

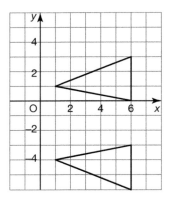

18

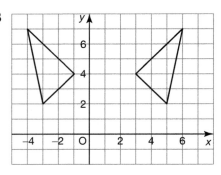

19 Draw △ABC by plotting A(1, 2), B(4, 1) and C(3, 4). Draw the image A′, B′, C′ when ABC is reflected in the *y*-axis.

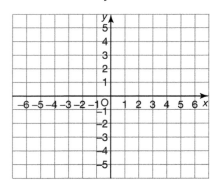

In questions **20** and **21**, write the equation of the mirror line.

20

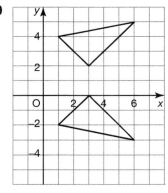

21

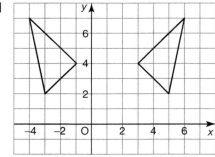

22 a Draw △XYZ where the vertices are the points X(−1, 4), Y(4, 4), Z(3, 1), and △X′Y′Z′ where the vertices are the points X′(−1, −2), Y′(4, −2), Z′(3, 1). Draw the mirror line so that △X′Y′Z′ is the reflection of △XYZ and write its equation.

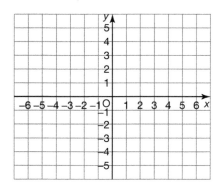

b Are there any invariant points? If so, name them.

23 a Draw △ABC where the vertices are the points A(3, 1), B(4, 4), C(1, 3), and △A′B′C′ where the vertices are the points A′(−1, −3), B′(−4, −4), C′(−3, −1). Draw the mirror line so that △A′B′C′ is the reflection of △ABC and write its equation.

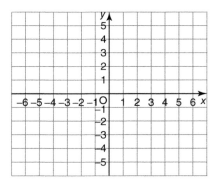

b Are there any invariant points? If so, name them.

_____

24 Write the following vectors in the form $\begin{pmatrix} p \\ q \end{pmatrix}$.

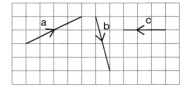

_____

_____

_____

25 Find the images of the given points under the translations described by the given vectors.

a $(4, 2), \begin{pmatrix} 3 \\ 6 \end{pmatrix}$ _____

b $(−3, 2), \begin{pmatrix} 3 \\ 5 \end{pmatrix}$ _____

c $(−2, −4), \begin{pmatrix} 6 \\ 1 \end{pmatrix}$ _____

d $(3, 5), \begin{pmatrix} −2 \\ −3 \end{pmatrix}$ _____

26 Find the vectors that describe the translations that map A to A′.

a A(2, 3), A′(5, 4) _____

b A(−2, 7), A′(4, 3) _____

c A(3, −4), A′(−2, −6) _____

d A(−3, −5), A′(2, −7) _____

27

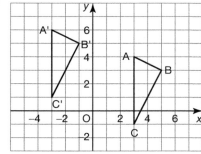

Given the above diagram, find the vectors:

$\overrightarrow{AA′} = \mathbf{a}$ _____

$\overrightarrow{BB′} = \mathbf{b}$ _____

$\overrightarrow{CC′} = \mathbf{c}$ _____

Are they all equal? _____

Is the transformation a translation? _____

28

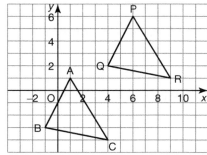

a Give the vectors describing the translations that map:

i △ABC to △PQR _____

ii △PQR to △ABC _____

b Plot the points X(1, 6), Y(3, 2), Z(–2, 1). Is the transformation that maps △XYZ to △PQR a translation or a reflection?

_____

If it is a translation, give the vector that describes it. If it is a reflection, give the equation of the mirror line.

_____

29

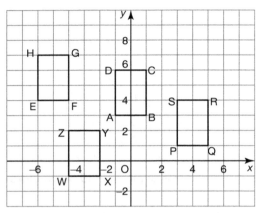

Give the vectors describing the translations that map:

a rectangle ABCD to rectangle EFGH

_____

b rectangle PQRS to rectangle EFGH

_____

c rectangle WXYZ to rectangle PQRS

_____

d rectangle ABCD to rectangle WXYZ.

_____

30

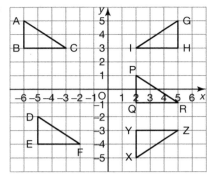

Describe fully the transformation that maps:

a triangle ABC to triangle DEF

_____

b triangle ABC to triangle GHI

_____

c triangle DEF to triangle PQR

_____

d triangle XYZ to triangle PQR

_____

e triangle ABC to triangle PQR

_____

f triangle PQR to triangle DEF.

_____

9 Measurement

1 Express the given quantity in terms of the unit in brackets:

a 7 m (cm) _____

b 12 km (m) _____

c 24 cm (mm) _____

d 56 km (cm) _____

e 7.4 m (cm) _____

f 6.2 m (mm) _____

g 3.4 cm (mm) _____

h 0.44 km (m) _____

2 Express the given quantity in terms of the unit in brackets:

a 4 kg (g) _____

b 15 t (kg) _____

c 40 g (mg) _____

d 3.5 t (kg) _____

e 0.4 g (mg) _____

f 1.8 kg (g) _____

g 0.7 g (mg) _____

h 0.8 kg (mg) _____

3 Express the given quantity in terms of the unit in brackets:

a 1 m 40 cm (cm) _____

b 5 cm 8 mm (mm) _____

c 6 m 55 cm (cm) _____

d 2 km 750 m (m) _____

e 7 g 500 mg (mg) _____

f 2 t 750 kg (kg) _____

g 4 kg 200 g (g) _____

h 1 kg 350 mg (mg) _____

4 Express the given quantity in terms of the unit in brackets:

a 700 mm (cm) _____

b 14 cm (m) _____

c 3450 m (km) _____

d 4 600 000 mm (km) _____

e 650 g (kg) _____

f 2200 mg (g) _____

g 2500 kg (t) _____

h 750 mg (g) _____

5 Express the given quantity in terms of the unit in brackets:

a 2 m 75 cm (cm) _____

b 7 km 40 m (km) _____

c 6 cm 8 mm (cm) _____

d 10 m 45 cm (m) _____

e 3 kg 443 g (kg) _____

f 7 kg 55 g (kg) _____

g 4 kg 89 g (g) _____

h 8 g 750 mg (mg) _____

6 Express the given quantity in terms of the unit in brackets:

a 7 m + 56 cm (m) _____

b 460 m + 3 km (km) _____

c 6 cm + 8 mm (cm) _____

d 550 mm + 46 cm + 2 m (m) _____

e 2 m + 34 cm (mm) _____

f 26 cm + 56 mm + 1 m (mm) _____

g 2.8 km + 290 m (m) _____

h 2 m + 39 cm + 600 mm (cm) _____

7 Express the given result in terms of the unit in brackets:

a 3t + 735 kg (kg)   _____

b 7 kg + 450 g (kg)   _____

c 44 kg + 0.3 t + 60 kg (kg)   _____

d 2.8 t + 56 kg (kg)   _____

e 3 m − 78 cm (cm)   _____

f 2.4 m − 845 mm (cm)   _____

g 2.5 t − 774 kg (kg)   _____

h 4.6 kg − 845 g (g)   _____

8 Calculate the following, giving your answer in the unit given in brackets:

a 5 × 2 kg 420 g (g)   _____

b 7 × 3 m 44 cm (m)   _____

c 3 × 5 km 340 m (km)   _____

9 Find, in metres, the perimeter of a rectangle in which the lengths of adjacent sides are 2.37 m and 560 cm.

_____

10 Find the total mass, in kilograms, of 750 g of mixed fruit, 675 g of flour and 460 g of butter.

_____

11 Find, in centimetres, the perimeter of a rectangular table cloth that is 510 mm long and 435 mm wide.

_____

12 A box contains 20 books, each weighing 500 g, and 10 books, each weighing 750 g.

Find the weight of books in the box.

_____

13 Express the given quantity in the unit in brackets:

a 8 yd 2 ft (ft)   _____

b 3 ft 4 in (in)   _____

c 1 mile 500 yd (yd)   _____

d 5 ft 7 in (in)   _____

14 Express the given quantity in the unit(s) in brackets:

a 48 in (ft)   _____

b 50 in (ft and in)   _____

c 15 ft (yd)   _____

d 70 ft (yd and ft)   _____

15 Express the given quantity in the unit(s) in brackets:

a 3 lb 8 oz (oz)   _____

b 2 tons 5 cwt (cwt)   _____

c 63 oz (lb and oz)   _____

d 160 lb (cwt and lb)   _____

16 Write the first unit roughly in terms of the unit in brackets:

a 4 kg (lb)   _____

b 10 lb (kg)   _____

c 50 miles (km)   _____

d 200 km (miles)   _____

17 Which is heavier:

a a 6 lb bag of carrots or a 4 kg bag of carrots

_____

b a 20 kg bag of cement or a 56 lb bag of cement?

_____

18 Which is the larger page size: one measuring 240 mm × 165 mm or 10 in × 7 in?

_____

19 The instructions for repotting a plant say that it should go in a 20 cm pot. The flower pots I have are marked 5 in, 8 in and 10 in. Which one should I use?

20

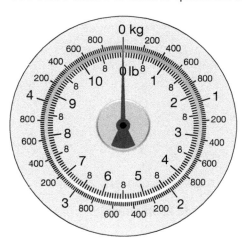

21 ft

33 ft

What, roughly, are the dimensions of this rectangle in metres?

Use these scales to answer questions **21** to **25**.

21 When the pointer is at 2 lb, what is the weight in grams? _____

22 When the pointer is at 1.1 kg, what is the weight in pounds and ounces?

23 When the pointer is at 5 lb, what is the weight in kilograms? _____

24 Find the number of grams in 1 lb.

25 Find the number of ounces in 500 g.

Use this ruler to answer questions **26** to **28**.

26 Find the number of centimetres in 5 inches.

27 Find the number of inches in 10 cm.

28 Find the number of millimetres in 2 inches.

29 The table shows the distance James walks in a given time.

Time in hours	1	$1\frac{1}{2}$	3	4	5
Distance in km	5	$7\frac{1}{2}$	15	20	25

Draw a graph showing these values.

Use a scale of 1 cm for 1 hour on the horizontal axis and 1 cm for 5 km on the vertical axis.

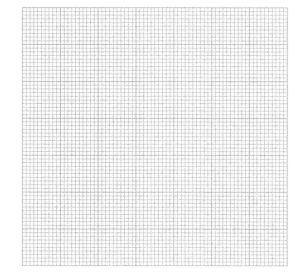

What do you notice about the speed at which James walks?

a How far has James walked:

   i in 2 hours   _____

   ii in $4\frac{1}{2}$ hours?   _____

b How long does it take him to walk:

   i 10 km   _____

   ii 12 km?   _____

30 The table shows the conversion of various sums of money from Canadian dollars to EC dollars.

Can$	50	100	150	200
EC$	128	256	384	512

Plot these points on a graph and draw a straight line to pass through them.

Let 1 cm represent 50 units on the horizontal Can$ axis and 1 cm represent 100 units on the EC$ axis.

Use your graph to convert:

a Can$70 to EC$ _____

b EC$350 to Can$ _____

c EC$430 to Can$ _____

d Can$180 to EC$.   _____

31 The table shows the conversion from miles to kilometres for various distances.

Miles	0	50	100
Kilometres	0	80	160

Plot these points on a graph and draw a straight line to pass through them.

Let 1 cm represent 25 units on both axes.

Use your graph to convert:

a 30 miles to kilometres

_____

b 100 km to miles

_____

c 140 km to miles

_____

d 75 miles to kilometres.

_____

32 The possible marks in a geography examination range from 0 to 55.
The table shows how some of the marks convert into percentages.

Mark	0	33	55
Percentage	0	60	100

Plot these points on a graph and draw a straight line to pass through them.
Choose your own scales.

Use your graph to express:

a a mark of 44 as a percentage

_____

b a mark of 25 as a percentage

_____

c the mark that gave 40%

_____

d the mark that gave 90%.

_____

33 The table shows the fuel consumption for Kayrel's car in kilometres per litre and in miles per imperial gallon.

km/l (*X*)	10	15	20
m.p.g. (*Y*)	28.6	42.9	57.1

Plot these points on a graph and draw a straight line through them.
Let 2 cm represent 4 units for *X* and 1 cm represent 10 units for *Y*.

Use your graph to convert:

a 12 km/l into m.p.g.

_____

b 18 m.p.g. into km/l

_____

c 35 m.p.g. into km/l

_____

d 18 km/l into m.p.g.

_____

1 Using $\pi = 3.142$ as an approximate value for π and giving your answers correct to 3 s.f., find the circumference of a circle of radius:

a 4.5 cm   _____

b 2.8 m   _____

c 470 mm   _____

d 0.076 km.   _____

2 Using $\pi = 3.14$ as an approximate value for π and giving your answers correct to 2 s.f., find the circumference of a circle of:

a radius 136 mm   _____

b diameter 7.8 m   _____

c diameter 530 cm   _____

d diameter 0.34 km.   _____

3 Find the perimeter of each of the following shapes. Use the value of π on your calculator. Give answers correct to 3 s.f.

a

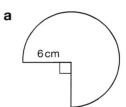

_____

b

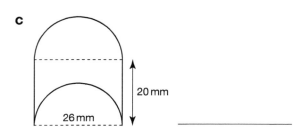

_____

c

_____

d

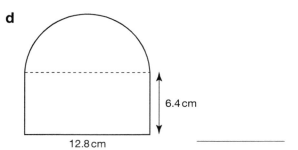

_____

e

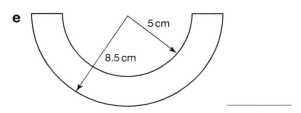

_____

4 Using 3.142 as the value of π and giving each answer correct to 3 s.f., find the value of the circumference of a wheel of:

a diameter 54 cm   _____

b radius 345 mm.   _____

For the questions that follow use the value of π on your calculator. Give each answer correct to 3 s.f.

5 A circular kitchen table of diameter 96 cm has a plastic strip around its edge. How long is the strip?

_____

6 The diameter of a coin is 30 mm. Find its circumference.

_____

7 Find the radius of a circle whose circumference is:

a 500 cm

_____

b 261 m.

_____

8 A water engineer uses a trundle
wheel to check the length of
a trench in which a new water
pipe has been laid. He pushes
the wheel over the smooth flat
surface after the work has been
completed.

a If the radius of the wheel is 10 cm, find its
circumference.

_____

b The wheel rotates 125 times. In metres,
how long is the trench?

_____

c He wishes to mark out the next 80 metres
of the pipe to be laid. How many rotations
of the trundle wheel must he count to
measure this distance?

_____

9 Find the area of a circle of:

a radius 7 cm   _____

b diameter 15 cm   _____

c radius 4.62 m.   _____

10 Find the area of each shape in question **3**.

a _____

b _____

c _____

d _____

e _____

11 The largest possible circle is cut from a square
of side 12 cm. Work out the area of paper that
is wasted.

_____

12 The diagram shows the stone entrance to a
tunnel.

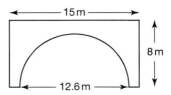

Find:

a the perimeter of the stone area

_____

b the area of the entrance to the tunnel

_____

c the surface area of the stone.

_____

13 The diagram shows the plan of a toy castle that
has identical towers at the corners. The curved
outline of each tower is three-quarters of a circle.

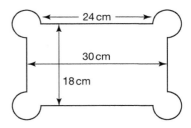

Find:

a the radius of one of these circles

_____

b the perimeter of the castle

_____

c the area of the castle.

_____

14 A cylindrical water tank is 1.22 m high and has a radius of 54 cm. Find:

a the distance around the circular base of the tank

_____

b the curved surface area of the tank

_____

c the total surface area of the tank.

_____

15 AB is the arc of a circle, centre O, of radius 6 cm. If angle AOB is 60°, find the length of the arc.

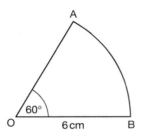

_____

16 The diagram shows a square of sheet metal of side 30 cm from which a circular piece of diameter 20 cm has been removed. Find the area of the remaining sheet.

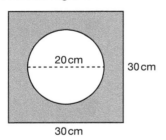

_____

17 The distance around the outer edge of a soup dish is 125 cm and the distance around the inner edge is 109 cm. Find:

a the diameter of the outer edge

_____

b the diameter of the inner edge

_____

c the width of the rim.

_____

18 The minute hand of the town clock is 1.4 metres long while the hour hand is 0.91 metres long.

a How far does the tip of the hour hand move in one hour?

_____

b How far does the tip of the minute hand move in one hour?

_____

19 A circular kitchen table, with a diameter of 90 cm, is covered by a circular tablecloth of diameter 114 cm.

Find the area of the cloth not in contact with the flat surface of the top of the table.

_____

20 The diagram below represents one of the windows in the town hall. Its shape is a square, of side 140 cm, surmounted by a semicircle.

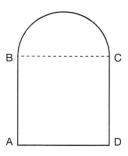

a Write:

i the length AB

_____

ii the length AD.

_____

b Find:

i the radius of the semicircle

_____

ii the length of the arc BC

_____

iii the height of the window.

_____

c What is the distance around the outside of the window?

_____

d Find the area of the window in square metres.

_____

21 Tim makes a telephone shelf that fits into a corner in the hall. It consists of two quadrants of plywood supported by two rectangular pieces, each of which can be screwed to the wall. The telephone rests on the top and the directories can be kept on the shelf beneath.

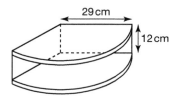

Use the dimensions given on the diagram to find:

a the area of one quadrant

_____

b the total area of plywood used to make this corner unit.

_____

In the remaining questions choose the letter that gives the correct answer. Each possible answer is given correct to 3 s.f.

In questions **22** to **24**, use $\pi = 3.142$

22 The circumference of a circle of radius 8.4 cm is:

A 5.28 cm   **B** 26.4 cm

C 52.7 cm   **D** 52.8 cm

23 The circumference of a circle with diameter 7.2 m is:

A 22.6 m   **B** 22.7 m

C 45.2 m   **D** 81.4 m

24 The circumference of a circle is 20 cm. Its radius is:

A 3.17 cm   **B** 3.18 cm

C 3.19 cm   **D** 3.20 cm

In the remaining questions, use the value of π on your calculator.

25 The area of a circle of radius 5.2 cm is:

   A 84.7 cm^2 **B** 84.8 cm^2

   C 84.9 cm^2 **D** 85.0 cm^2

26 The area of a circle whose diameter is 15 cm is:

   A 175 cm^2 **B** 176 cm^2

   C 177 cm^2 **D** 707 cm^2

27 The area of a circle is 100 cm^2. Its radius is:

   A 5.73 cm   **B** 5.64 cm

   C 11.2 cm   **D** 11.3 cm

28 The largest possible circle is drawn to fit into a square of side 25 cm. The distance around the square is greater than the distance around the circle by:

   A 20.5 cm   **B** 21.5 cm

   C 25 cm   **D** 25.6 cm

29 The diameters of three different sizes of plates in a dinner service are 16 cm, 21 cm and 27 cm. How much further is it around the edge of the largest plate compared with the distance around the edge of the smallest plate?

   A 34.5 cm   **B** 34.6 cm

   C 34.8 cm   **D** 34.9 cm

1 Find the volume of a cuboid measuring 12 cm by 8 cm by 5 cm.

2 Find the volume of a cuboid measuring 250 cm by 40 cm by 20 cm.

In questions **3** to **7**, find the volumes of the following cuboids. Do not draw a diagram. The table gives the units to use for your answer, so convert the units first, if necessary.

	Length	Width	Height	Volume
3	24 cm	5 cm	6 cm	cm^3
4	11.2 cm	0.5 cm	30 mm	cm^3
5	25 mm	12 mm	8 mm	cm^3
6	0.35 m	2.8 m	25 cm	cm^3
7	8.6 m	3.5 m	1.6 m	m^3

In questions **8** to **11**, find the volumes of the prisms. Draw a diagram of the cross-section but do not draw a picture of the solid.

8

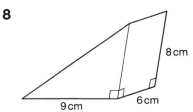

9

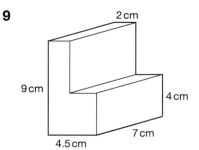

10

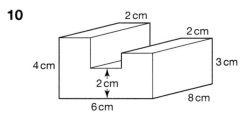

11

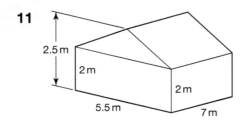

14

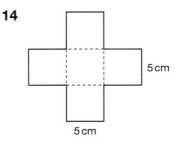

Length 3.5 cm

In questions **12** to **16**, the cross-sections of the prisms and their lengths are given. Find their volumes.

12

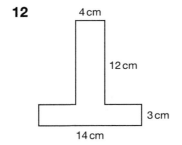

Length 12 cm

15

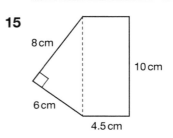

Length 8 cm

13

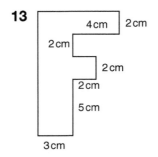

Length 8 cm

16

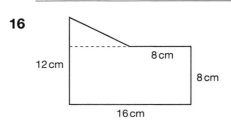

Length 12 cm

In questions **17** to **23**, use the value of π on your calculator and give all your answers correct to 3 s.f.

Find the volumes of cylinders with the following dimensions:

17 radius 4 cm, height 6 cm　　　　————————

18 radius 6 cm, height 5.5 cm　　　————————

19 radius 3.5 cm, height 7.5 cm　　————————

20 diameter 8 cm, height 3.6 cm　　————————

21 diameter 3.8 cm, height 3 cm　　————————

22 radius 9.4 cm, height 5.3 cm　　————————

23 diameter 0.4 m, height 0.15 m　————————

In questions **24** to **28**, find the volumes of the following solids. Use the value of π on your calculator and give all your answers correct to 3 s.f.

24 A solid is made of two cylinders each of height 6 cm. The radius of the smaller cylinder is 3 cm and the radius of the larger cylinder is 5 cm.

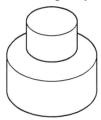

25 A solid wheel of radius 9 cm and thickness 4 cm is fixed on an axle of radius 1 cm and length 30 cm.

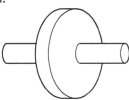

26 A solid is 12 cm long. Its cross-section is a rectangle measuring 8 cm by 2 cm surmounted by a semicircle.

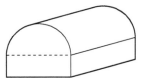

27 A solid, whose cross-section is a rectangle 12 cm by 3 cm with semicircles on opposite faces, is 30 cm long.

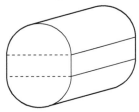

28 The diagram shows a rectangular block measuring 10 cm by 8 cm by 6 cm from which a semicircular channel of diameter 4 cm has been removed.

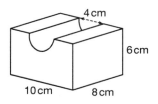

29 The length of the side of a cube is 3 cm.

a What is the total surface area of this cube?

b What is the sum of the lengths of all the edges of this cube?

c How many cubes of side 1 cm are needed to fill the same space as the given cube?

30 A cuboid is 6 m long, 80 cm wide and 60 cm wide. Find:

a its total surface area in square metres

b its volume in cubic metres.

31 A book of puzzles measures 20 cm by 12 cm by 3 cm. A shopkeeper takes delivery of a carton of these books measuring 60 cm by 24 cm by 9 cm. How many books are packed in a carton?

In the remaining questions choose the letter that gives the correct answer.

32 When $3.2\,m^3$ is expressed in cubic centimetres the value is:

A $32\,000\,cm^3$ **B** $320\,000\,cm^3$

C $3\,200\,000\,cm^3$ **D** $32\,000\,000\,cm^3$

33 1.6 litres, expressed in cubic centimetres is:

A $160\,cm^3$ **B** $1600\,cm^3$

C $16\,000\,cm^3$ **D** $160\,000\,cm^3$

34 The volume of a cube of side 4 cm is:

A $16\,cm^3$ **B** $32\,cm^3$

C $64\,cm^3$ **D** $128\,cm^3$

35 The volume of a cuboid measuring 2 m by 25 cm by 10 cm is:

A $0.05\,m^3$ **B** $0.5\,m^3$

C $5\,m^3$ **D** $50\,m^3$

36 The volume of a cuboid measuring 5 cm by 3 cm by 9 mm is:

A $13.5\,mm^3$ **B** $135\,mm^3$

C $1350\,mm^3$ **D** $13\,500\,mm^3$

37

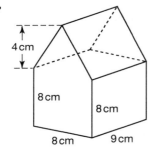

The volume of this prism is:

A $504\,cm^3$ **B** $704\,cm^3$

C $720\,cm^3$ **D** $792\,cm^3$

38 The capacity, in litres, of a rectangular tank measuring 3 m by 2 m by 80 cm is:

A 480 litres   **B** 4800 litres

C 48 000 litres   **D** 480 000 litres

39 The volume, in cubic metres, of a cylinder of radius 40 cm and height 2 m is:

A $0.32\pi\,m^3$ **B** $3.2\pi\,m^3$

C $32\pi\,m^3$ **D** $320\pi\,m^3$

40 The volume of a circular disc, radius 3 cm and thickness 6 mm is:

A $5.4\pi\,cm^3$ **B** $54\pi\,mm^3$

C $54\pi\,cm^3$ **D** $540\pi\,mm^3$

41

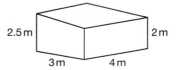

The amount of space within this glasshouse is:

A $24\,m^3$ **B** $26\,m^3$

C $27\,m^3$ **D** $30\,m^3$

1

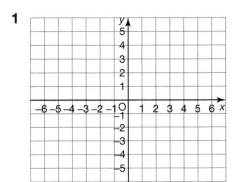

a Mark the points A(3, 4), B(5, –2), C(–3, –2) and D(–5, 4) on the grid. Join the points to form the special quadrilateral ABCD. Name the type of quadrilateral.

_____

b Join AC and BD. Mark the point E where these diagonals cross. Write the coordinates of E.

_____

2 A, B, C and D are points on the same straight line.

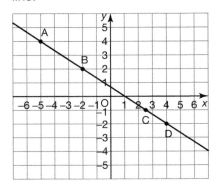

a Write the coordinates of A, B, C and D.

A(,   ),   B(,   ),
C(,   ),   D(,   )

b E is another point on this line.
Its x-coordinate is 1. Write its y-coordinate.

_____

c Find the gradient of the line.

_____

3 **a** Complete the following table for the line $y = -2x + 1$

x	–2	0	2
y			

b Draw the graph of $y = -2x + 1$

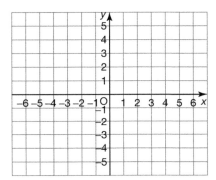

4 For the following equations of straight lines write:

i the gradient m **ii** the y-intercept:

a $y = 7x - 3$

i _____   ii _____

b $y = -2x + 1$

i _____   ii _____

c $\frac{1}{3}x - 6$

i _____   ii _____

5 Write the equations of the straight lines that have the given gradient and y-intercept.

a gradient 5, y-intercept –2

_____

b gradient –3, y-intercept –1

_____

c gradient $-\dfrac{2}{3}$, y-intercept $\dfrac{1}{3}$

_____

6 Represent the region described by the following inequalities:

$3 \leqslant x, \quad -2 \leqslant y < 4$

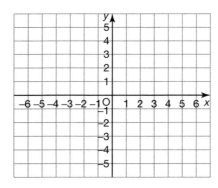

7 Complete the drawing so that the broken lines are lines of symmetry.

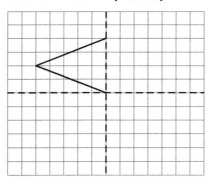

8 Draw the reflection of the object in the mirror line and label the image A′B′C′.

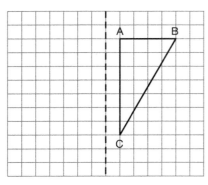

9 Write the equation of the mirror line.

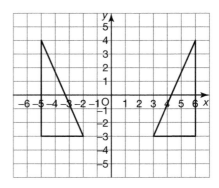

_____

10 Write the vectors **a**, **b**, **c** in the form $\begin{pmatrix} p \\ q \end{pmatrix}$

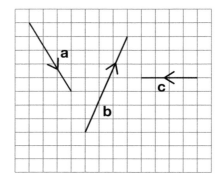

a _____   **b** _____   **c** _____

11

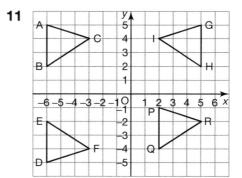

Describe fully the transformation that maps:

a triangle ABC to triangle GHI

_____

b triangle PQR to triangle ABC

_____

c triangle DEF to triangle ABC.

12 Express the given quantity in terms of the unit in brackets.

a 1.5 m (cm) _____

b 1.4 kg (g) _____

c 1065 g (kg) _____

d 540 mm (cm) _____

e 5050 kg (t) _____

13 Find in kilograms the total mass of 540 g of sugar, 380 g of flour and 890 g of butter.

14 A box contains 50 tins of tomatoes; each tin weighs 250 g. The box weighs 400 g. Find, in kilograms, the total weight of the box and tins of tomatoes.

15 Express the given quantity in terms of the unit in brackets.

a 44 in (feet and inches) _____

b 4 ft 5 in (inches) _____

c 36 oz (pounds and ounces) _____

d 1 ton 2 cwt (cwt) _____

16 Which is longer:

a 15 in or 45 cm _____

b 16 miles or 20 km? _____

17 Which is heavier:

a 2 kg or 6 lb _____

b 5 oz or 200 g? _____

18 Using your calculator and giving your answers correct to 3 s.f., find the circumference of a circle of:

a radius 6.6 cm _____

b diameter 45 m _____

19 Find the perimeter of each shape, giving your answer correct to 3 s.f.

a

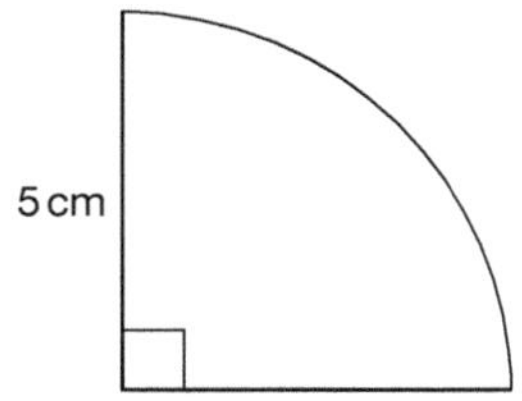

5 cm

b

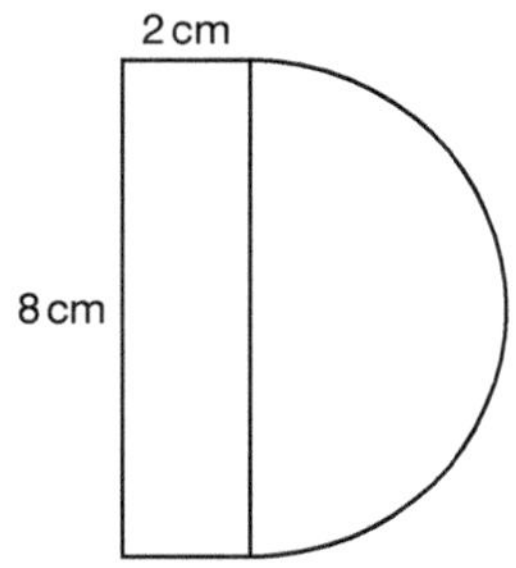

2 cm

8 cm

20 Find, correct to 3 s.f., the area of a circle of:

a radius 8 m _____

b diameter 36 cm _____

21 Find the area of each shape in question **19**.

a _____

b _____

22 The diagram shows a square washer of side 6 mm with a circular hole of diameter 4 mm removed from its centre. Find the area of the material from which the washer is made (the shaded area).

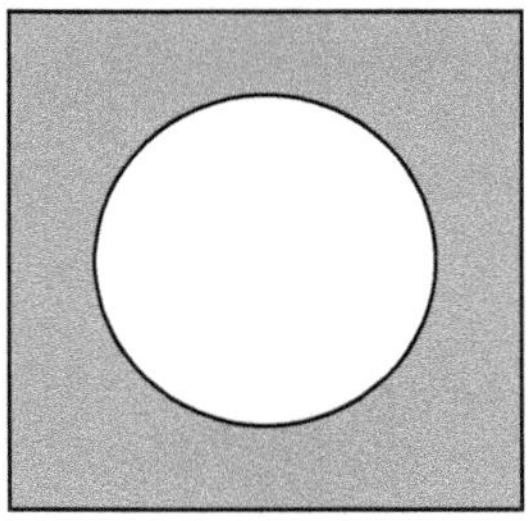

23 Find the volume of a cube whose edges are 1.5 cm.

_____

24 Find the volume of a cuboid measuring 3 cm by 5 cm by 9 cm.

_____

25 Find the volume of a cuboid with a square cross-section of side 3 mm and which is 10 mm long.

_____

26 Find the volume of each prism:

a

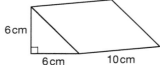

_____

b

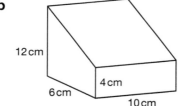

_____

27 A cylinder has a circular cross-section of diameter 20 cm and is 45 cm long. Find the volume of the cylinder.

_____

For the remaining questions, choose the letter that gives the correct answer.

28 The gradient of the line $y = 3 - 2x$ is:

A −3 **B** −2

C 2 **D** 3

29 The line with equation $y = 5x - 1$ cuts the y-axis at the point:

A (5, 0) **B** (0, 5)

C (1, 0) **D** (0, −1)

30 In mm, 0.5 m is:

A 5 **B** 50

C 500 **D** 5000

31 The approximate number of pounds equivalent to 5 kg is:

A 0.5 **B** 2.5

C 5 **D** 10

32 The circumference of a circle with a diameter of 3 cm is:

A 1.5π **B** 3π

C 6π **D** 9π

33 The area of a circle with a diameter of 3 cm is:

A 2.25π **B** 3π

C 6π **D** 9π

34 The vector in the diagram is:

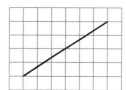

A $\begin{pmatrix} 4 \\ 6 \end{pmatrix}$ **B** $\begin{pmatrix} 6 \\ 4 \end{pmatrix}$

C $\begin{pmatrix} 4 \\ 4 \end{pmatrix}$ **D** $\begin{pmatrix} 6 \\ 6 \end{pmatrix}$

35 The volume of a cuboid measuring 4 cm by 5 cm by 6 cm is:

A 120 cm³ **B** 60 cm³

C 15 cm³ **D** 6 cm³

12   Ratio and proportion

1 Express the following ratios in their simplest form:

   a 10:12 _____

   b 40:30 _____

   c 35:42 _____

   d 5 cm:20 cm _____

   e 64c:88c _____

   f 85 g:1 kg _____

   g 32c:$1.92 _____

   h 270:525 _____

2 Express the following ratios in their simplest form:

   a 10 cm:50 mm _____

   b $50\,cm^2:2\,m^2$ _____

   c 12:16:20 _____

   d 9:3:12 _____

   e 15:25:45 _____

   f 35:21:14 _____

   g 147:189:63 _____

3 Express the following ratios in their simplest form:

   a $7:\dfrac{2}{3}$ _____

   b $\dfrac{3}{4}:2$ _____

   c $\dfrac{1}{6}:\dfrac{1}{3}$ _____

   d $\dfrac{1}{4}:\dfrac{1}{2}$ _____

   e $\dfrac{4}{5}:3$ _____

   f $4:\dfrac{7}{10}$ _____

   g $\dfrac{5}{9}:\dfrac{2}{3}$ _____

   h $\dfrac{1}{2}:\dfrac{2}{3}:\dfrac{7}{12}$ _____

   i $\dfrac{5}{24}:\dfrac{7}{12}:\dfrac{5}{6}$ _____

4 Express the following ratios in their simplest form:

   a $\dfrac{2}{5}:\dfrac{1}{3}$ _____

   b $\dfrac{3}{8}:2$ _____

   c $1\tfrac{1}{2}:5$ _____

   d $\tfrac{1}{2}:2\tfrac{1}{4}$ _____

   e $1\tfrac{1}{3}:1\tfrac{1}{5}$ _____

   f 1.2:0.6 _____

   g 3.2:1.8 _____

   h 1 cm:5 mm _____

   i 2.14 cm:58 mm _____

5 Which is the larger?

   a 5:6 or 3:4 _____

   b 8:7 or 15:14 _____

   c 2:7 or $\dfrac{3}{5}$ _____

6 Which is the smaller?

   a 9:7 or 13:11 _____

   b $\dfrac{3}{4}$ or $\dfrac{5}{7}$ _____

   c 1.5:2.5 or 3.2:4.8 _____

7 On a shelf there are 24 red books and 32 green books. What is the ratio of:

   a green books to red books ＿＿＿＿＿＿

   b red books to green books. ＿＿＿＿＿＿

8 In a school sports' team there are 21 girls and 14 boys. Find the ratio of:

   a boys to girls   ＿＿＿＿＿＿

   b girls to children.   ＿＿＿＿＿＿

9 Peter has three sisters and four brothers. Including himself, find the ratio of:

   a brothers to sisters   ＿＿＿＿＿＿

   b sisters to children.   ＿＿＿＿＿＿

10 A bunch of flowers contains five white flowers, three red flowers and seven yellow flowers. Find the ratio of:

   a red flowers to yellow flowers ＿＿＿＿

   b white flowers to red flowers ＿＿＿＿

   c white flowers to all the flowers in the bunch. ＿＿＿＿＿＿

11 A rectangular scarf is 1.5 m long and 30 cm wide. Find the ratio of:

   a the length of the scarf to its width

   ＿＿＿＿＿＿＿＿＿＿＿＿＿＿＿＿

   b the length of the scarf to its perimeter.

   ＿＿＿＿＿＿＿＿＿＿＿＿＿＿＿＿

12 Newbridge School has 180 pupils. To get to school, 60 pupils cycle, 36 come by bus and the remainder walk. Find the ratio of:

   a the number who cycle to the number who come by bus ＿＿＿＿＿＿＿＿

   b the number who walk to the number who cycle ＿＿＿＿＿＿＿＿

   c the number who walk to the number of pupils in the school. ＿＿＿＿＿＿

13 The perimeter of a rectangle is 28 cm. Find the ratio of its length to its width if it is 6 cm wide.

＿＿＿＿＿＿＿＿＿＿＿＿＿＿＿＿＿＿

14 Toothpaste is sold in three sizes—standard, large and family.

What is the ratio of:

   a the cost of the family size to the cost of the standard size

   ＿＿＿＿＿＿＿＿＿＿＿＿＿＿＿

   b the cost of the large size to the cost of the family size

   ＿＿＿＿＿＿＿＿＿＿＿＿＿＿＿

   c the mass of the large size to the mass of the standard size

   ＿＿＿＿＿＿＿＿＿＿＿＿＿＿＿

   d the mass of the standard size to the mass of the family size?

   ＿＿＿＿＿＿＿＿＿＿＿＿＿＿＿

15 A brand of instant coffee is sold in three sizes.

Find the ratio of:

   a the mass of the 100 g pack to the mass of the 250 g pack

   ＿＿＿＿＿＿＿＿＿＿＿＿＿＿＿

b the cost of the 250 g pack to the 100 g pack

_____

c the mass of the 1 kg pack to the mass of the 250 g pack

_____

d the cost of the 1 kg pack to the cost of the 250 g pack.

_____

16 Find the missing numbers in the following ratios:

a $3:4 = 6:$ _____

b $7:3 = 21:$ _____

c $\dfrac{}{2} = \dfrac{12}{4}$ _____

d $\dfrac{3}{4} = \dfrac{15}{}$ _____

e $\dfrac{5}{9} = \dfrac{}{36}$ _____

f $:24 = 8:12$ _____

g $2:8 = 12:$ _____

h $21:49 = \ :7$ _____

17 Find the value of x in each of the following:

a $\dfrac{x}{2} = \dfrac{5}{8}$ _____

b $\dfrac{x}{7} = \dfrac{4}{5}$ _____

c $x:4 = 9:12$ _____

d $x:5 = 10:25$ _____

e $x:3 = 49:21$ _____

f $8:14 = x:7$ _____

g $72:16 = 18:x$ _____

18 Find the missing numbers in the following ratios:

a $:7 = 5:4$ _____

b $:6 = 2:5$ _____

c $:3 = 6:5$ _____

d $10: \ = 12:7$ _____

e $7: \ = 5:8$ _____

f $:4 = 4:3$ _____

g $:3 = 8:7$ _____

h $4:5 = 3:$ _____

19 Two masses are in the ratio $5:7$. The second mass is 42 kg. Find the first mass.

_____

20 In a rectangle, the ratio of the length to the width is $9:5$. If the length is 36 cm find the width.

_____

21 The ratio of the perimeter of a triangle to its longest side is $9:4$. The perimeter is 27 cm. What is the length of the longest side?

_____

22 The ratio of the length of a model motorcar to the actual car is $1:50$. The car is 4.55 m long. How long is the model?

_____

23 Two lengths are in the ratio $3:10$. The shorter length is 12 cm. Find the longer length.

_____

24 The ratio of the area of two fields is $5:16$. The area of the larger field is 4800 m². Find the area of the smaller field.

_____

25 a Divide 90c into two parts in the ratio $4:5$.

_____

b Divide 125 cm into two parts in the ratio 2:3.

_____

c Divide 117 g into two parts in the ratio 6:7.

_____

26 a Divide 150 grams into two parts in the ratio 3:2.

_____

b Divide $100 dollars into two parts in the ratio 3:7.

_____

c Divide 750 sweets into two parts in the ratio 3:5.

_____

27 In a debating society meeting, the ratio of the number of pupils voting for the motion to the number of pupils voting against the motion is 8:7. If 195 pupils voted, how many voted against the motion?

_____

28 The ratio of the length of a room to its width is 4:3. The room is 6 metres long.

a How wide is it?

_____

b What is the area of the room?

_____

29 The scale used to make a model of a railway engine is 1:72.

a If the engine is 7.2 m long, how long is the model?

_____

b One wheel on the model has a diameter of 1.5 cm. Find, in metres, the diameter of the wheel on the engine?

_____

30 Divide $162 between Liz and Denis in the ratio 5:4.

_____

31 Divide 143 m in the ratio 3:8.

_____

32 April and Dylan share a box of sweets in the ratio 3:2. April gets 10 more sweets than Dylan. How many sweets were in the box?

_____

33 Peter and Jayne each have their own bedroom. The ratio of the area of Peter's room to Jayne's room is 6:8. The area of Jayne's room is 2 m² greater than the area of Peter's room. Find the area of Peter's room.

_____

34 The number of pages in a book with pictures on them is $\frac{2}{5}$ of the total number of pages. What is the ratio of the number of pages with pictures to the number of pages without pictures?

_____

35 Find the map ratio if:

a 2 cm on the map represents 500 m

_____

b the scale of the map is 1 cm to 4 km

_____

c 10 km is represented by 5 cm on the map

_____

d 5 cm on the map represents 100 m

e 100 m is represented by 4 cm

_____

f the scale of the map is 1 cm to 100 m.

_____

36 The scale of a map is 1 : 10 000.

    a What distance, in metres, does 12 cm on the map represent?

    _____

    b What distance on the map represents a distance of 5 km?

    _____

37 The scale of a map is 1 : 50 000.

    a What distance, in metres, does 1 cm on the map represent?

    _____

    b What distance, in kilometres, does 10 cm on the map represent?

    _____

    c Two villages are 2 km apart. How far apart will they be on the map?

    _____

38 If 3 m of material costs $64.80 how much will 7 m cost?

_____

39 Lisa earns $22 in 4 hours. How much will she earn:

    a in 1 hour   _____

    b in 36 hours?   _____

40 A recipe for 15 rich cakes includes 100 g sugar and 200 g flour.

    a How much of each ingredient would be needed to make 30 of these cakes?

    _____

b If 600 g of flour is used, how many cakes would you expect?

_____

c Sugar costs $2.70 a kilogram. How much would the sugar cost for 45 cakes?

_____

41 A recipe for pizza to serve four people includes 145 g of plain flour, 90 millilitres of milk and 115 g of tinned tomatoes. How much of each ingredient would be required to make a pizza to serve:

    a 8 people _____

    b 12 people? _____

42 A truck travels 100 km on 20 litres of gas.

    a How far will it travel on 55 litres of gas?

    _____

    b How many litres of gas are needed for a journey of 550 km?

    _____

43 Oranges are sold by weight with 500 g of oranges costing $20.00. How much will 2 kg of these oranges cost?

_____

44 A model of a ship is made to a scale of 1 : 250. The length of model is 20 cm. How long is the length of the model?

_____

45 A tower is 40 m tall. A scale model of the tower is 40 cm tall.

    a Find the scale used to make the model.

    _____

    b The diameter of the base of the tower is 6 m. What is the diameter of the base of the model?

    _____

46 State whether each of the following are in direct proportion. Give a brief reason for your answer.

   a The number of bananas bought to the cost of the bananas.

   _____

   b The number of socks in a drawer to the number of pairs of socks in the drawer.

   _____

   c At a constant speed, the distance walked and the time taken.

   _____

   d The distance walked and the speed walked at constant speed.

   _____

   e The number of people in a queue and the time taken to get to the front of the queue.

   _____

47 Andres walks at 4 km/h. Draw a graph to show him walking for three hours. Take 1 cm to represent 1 km and 4 cm to represent one hour. Use your graph to find how far he walks in:

   a $1\frac{1}{2}$ hours   _____

   b $2\frac{1}{4}$ hours.   _____

48 A bus travels at 44 km/h. How far will it travel in:

   a 2 hours   _____

   b 5 hours   _____

   c $3\frac{1}{2}$ hours   _____

   d $2\frac{1}{4}$ hours?   _____

49 Lorna can cycle at 18 km/h. How far will she ride in:

   a $\dfrac{1}{2}$ hour   _____

   b 20 minutes   _____

   c $1\frac{1}{2}$ hours   _____

   d 1 hour 40 minutes?   _____

50 An aeroplane flies at 360 mph. How far will it fly in:

   a 6 hours   _____

   b $7\frac{1}{2}$ hours   _____

   c $9\frac{1}{4}$ hours?   _____

51 A racing car travels at 90 mph. How far will it travel in:

   a $1\frac{1}{2}$ hours   _____

   b 45 minutes   _____

   c 12 minutes?   _____

52 How long will it take a car travelling at 70 km/h to travel:

   a 140 km   _____

   b 35 km   _____

   c 175 km?   _____

53 How long will it take an aeroplane travelling at 360 mph to travel:

   a 900 miles   _____

   b 540 miles   _____

   c 2070 miles?   _____

54 A sprinter runs at 10 m/sec. How long will it take him to run:

   a 60 metres   _____

   b 100 metres?   _____

55 A ship travels at 12 nautical miles per hour. How long will it take to travel:

   a 240 nautical miles   _____

   b 2880 nautical miles   _____

   c 2016 nautical miles?   _____

56 A car travels at 88 km/h.
How long will it take to travel:

   a 220 km   _____

   b 242 km   _____

   c 330 km?   _____

57 Kenneth cycles at 18 km/h.
How long will it take him to cycle:

   a 54 km   _____

   b 45 km   _____

   c 66 km?   _____

58 Miranda drives at 60 mph.

   a How long will it take her to drive 90 miles?

   b How far can she travel in $2\frac{1}{2}$ hours?

   c How long will it take her to drive 50 miles?

   d How far can she travel in 40 minutes?

59 An airliner cruises at 540 km/h.

   a How long will it take to fly 1080 km?

   b How long will it take to fly 2000 km?

60 A car ferry travels at 25 km/h.

   a How far will it travel in 1.5 hours?

   b How long will it take to travel 10 km?

61 A formula 1 car can travel at 200 km/h.
At this speed:

   a how long will it take to cover 0.5 km

   b how far can it travel in 12 seconds?

62 A car is travelling at a constant speed of 40 km/h.

   a How far will it travel in 30 minutes?

   b How long will it take to travel 30 km?

63 A car is travelling at 60 km/h when the driver sees a fallen tree in the road. The tree is 100 m in front of the car. Assuming that the driver does not brake, how long will it take for the car to hit the tree?

64 Kemar cycles at 20 km/h.

   a How long will it take him to cycle 45 km?

   b How far can he cycle in $1\frac{1}{4}$ hours?

   c How long will it take him to cycle 85 km?

   d How far can he travel in 45 minutes?

65 Mushad walks at 6 km/h.

  a How far can he walk in 20 minutes?

  _____

  b If Mushad only walks at 4 km/h, how much longer will it take him to walk the same distance?

  _____

66 Find the average speed for each of the following journeys:

  a 160 km in 4 hours _____

  b 60 miles in 2 hours _____

  c 105 m in 3 seconds _____

  d 180 km in 3 hours _____

  e 315 m in 9 seconds. _____

67 Find the average speed in km/h for a journey of:

  a 50 km in 30 minutes _____

  b 40 km in 40 minutes _____

  c $10\frac{1}{2}$ km in 45 minutes. _____

68 Find the average speed in mph for a journey of:

  a 32 miles in 30 minutes _____

  b 90 miles in 45 minutes _____

  c $7\frac{1}{2}$ miles in 25 minutes. _____

69 Find the average speed in km/h for a journey of:

  a 40.5 km in 2 hours _____

  b 20 km in 0.25 hours _____

  c 2.6 km in 10 minutes _____

  d 0. 2 km in 30 seconds _____

70 The table shows the distances, in metres, between the garage (G), library (L), church (Ch), post office (PO), harbour (H), college (C) and school (S) in a town.

	G	L	Ch	PO	H	C
L	550					
Ch	600	400				
PO	550	1250	200			
H	350	550	750	700		
C	300	250	350	250	450	
S	450	300	600	650	300	250

Use this table to find the average speeds, in metres/minute, for journeys between:

  a the harbour and the library taking two minutes

  _____

  b the school and the college taking four minutes

  _____

  c the church and the school leaving at 10.44 a.m. and arriving at 10.49 a.m.

  _____

  d the harbour and the garage leaving at 11.55 a.m. and arriving at 12.07 p.m.

  _____

71 Charlee went for a walk. She walked 1.5 km in 20 minutes. She then had a rest for 5 minutes and continued her walk, going 1 km in 15 minutes.

  a How fast did she walk on the first section of her journey?

  _____

  b How fast did she walk on the last section of her journey?

  _____

  c How long did her walk take in total?

  _____

  d What was her average speed for the walk?

  _____

72 A car travelled at 45 km/h for 60 km. The car then turned round and drove back to its starting point, travelling at 60 km/h.

a How far did the car travel in total?

_____

b How long was the car travelling for?

_____

c What was the average speed of the car?

_____

73 Maria cycles to school. She cycles at 16 km/h for 20 minutes. She then stops for 10 minutes. Maria then cycles the remaining 2 km of her journey in 15 minutes.

a How far does Maria cycle before she stops?

_____

b What is Maria's speed for the last 15 minutes of her journey?

_____

c How far is the school from Maria's home?

_____

d Find Maria's average speed for the whole journey.

_____

74 Jason walks to school, a distance of 1.5 km. He walks for 300 m when he stops to talk to a friend. He then walks for 600 m when he meets another friend and stops to talk. Jason then walks the remaining distance to school. The walk from home to school takes Jason a total time of 45 minutes.

a What is Jason's average speed for his journey?

_____

b What average speed would Jason need so that he only takes 30 minutes to walk to school?

_____

75 The map ratio of a map is 1 : 50 000. On the map the distance between Newtown and Westly is 8 cm. What is the true distance between these two places?

_____

1 If a number is increased by the given percentage, what percentage is the new number of the original number?

a 40% _____

b 70% _____

c 55% _____

d 24% _____

e 200% _____

f $137\frac{1}{2}$% _____

2 Give the multiplying factor which increases a number by:

a 50% _____

b 35% _____

c 150% _____

d 400% _____

3 If a number is decreased by the given percentage, what percentage is the new number of the original number?

a 20% _____

b 75% _____

c 52% _____

d 48% _____

e 15% _____

f $66\frac{2}{3}$% _____

4 Give the multiplying factor which decreases a number by:

a 30% _____

b 65% _____

c 15% _____

d 40% _____

5 Increase:

a 60 by 50% _____

b 800 by 15% _____

c 36 by 350% _____

d 424 by 45% _____

6 Decrease:

a 6500 by 40% _____

b 220 by 65% _____

c 180 by 85% _____

d $12\frac{1}{2}$ by 40% _____

7 a Increase $160 by 40% _____

b Increase 36 kg by 35% _____

c Decrease $260 by 15% _____

d Decrease 54 cm by 50% _____

8 a Increase $2500 by 15% _____

b Decrease $205 000 by 8% _____

c Increase 1500 m by $12\frac{1}{2}$% _____

d Decrease 620 seconds by 80% _____

9 The price of a watch marked $60 rises by 12%. Find its new price.

_____

10 David's weekly income of $1980 increases by 15%. Find his new income.

_____

11 A boy's height increased by 20% from his twelfth to his fourteenth birthday. If he was 145 cm tall on his twelfth birthday how tall was he when he reached fourteen?

_____

12 Water increases in volume by 4% when frozen. Find the volume of $425\,cm^3$ water when converted into ice.

_____

13 A girl is 25% taller now than she was three years ago. Three years ago her height was $128\,cm$. How tall is she now?

_____

14 When carving a model a boy estimates that he will cut away 56% of the wood he starts with. He has a piece of wood with a mass of $2.5\,kg$. What will be the mass of his model?

_____

15 When it was washed, a cotton table cloth shrank by $2\frac{1}{2}$%. It was $2.40\,m$ long before it was washed. How long was it after it was washed?

_____

16 This year there were 720 students enrolled in a school. The number of students enrolled next year is expected to be 4% higher. Find the number of students expected to be on the school roll next year.

_____

17 Find the total hire purchase cost in each case.

a No deposit, 12 monthly payments of $350

_____

b No deposit, 12 monthly payments of $650

_____

c No deposit, 24 monthly payments of $8500

_____

d No deposit, 36 monthly payments of $180

_____

18 Find the total hire purchase cost in each case.

a Deposit of $9000 plus 12 monthly payments of $320

_____

b Deposit of $50 000 plus 12 monthly payments of $620

_____

c Deposit of $85 000 plus 12 monthly payments of $490

_____

d Deposit of $13 000 plus 24 monthly payments of $180

_____

e Deposit of $35 000 plus 36 monthly payments of $710

_____

19 The cash price of a tablet is $1050. If bought on hire purchase, a deposit of $105 is required followed by 24 monthly payments of $76. Find how much is saved by paying cash.

_____

20 Another tablet costs $1800 for cash. If bought on hire purchase, a deposit of 10% is required followed by 24 monthly payments of $110. Find how much is saved by paying cash.

_____

21 The cash price of a laptop is $4824. If bought on hire purchase, a deposit of 15% is required followed by 36 monthly payments of $145. Find how much is saved by paying cash.

_____

22 The price of a second-hand car is marked as $22 995. A discount of 3% is given if bought for cash. The hire purchase terms are a deposit of 10% of the marked price plus 12 monthly payments of $2500. Find the difference between the cash price and the amount paid for hire purchase.

23 A carpet is priced at $89.00 per square metre. Ravij needs 12 square metres to cover his living room. If he pays for it by hire purchase, the terms are 10% deposit plus six monthly payments of $420. How much cheaper is it to pay cash?

24 Ann Kanhai works a five-day week. She starts work each day at 7 a.m. and finishes at 4.10 p.m. She has 30 minutes for lunch and a 15 minute break both morning and afternoon.

   a How long does she actually work:

      i in a day

      ii in a week?

   b If her hourly rate is $40.80, calculate her gross wage for the week.

25 Ceejay starts work at 7 a.m. and finishes at 3.30 p.m. He has an unpaid lunch break of one hour.

   a How many paid hours does he work in a five-day week?

   b He is paid $40 an hour. Find his gross weekly pay.

26 Priscilla Weaver works in a business where the basic hourly rate is $6.40 for a 35-hour week. Any overtime is paid at time-and-a-half. How much will she earn in a week when she works 46 hours?

27 Last week Nora Raman worked eight hours from Monday to Friday and also 5 hours on Saturday. The normal working day is seven hours and time worked in excess of this is paid at time-and-a-half, with Saturday working paid at double-time. Work out her gross pay for the week if her basic hourly rate is $13.08.

28 Leela is paid $10.50 for each hour for a normal working week of 36 hours. She is paid time-and-a-half for each hour she works over 36 hours.

   a Find her gross weekly pay for a normal working week.

   b Find her gross pay for a week in which she works 48 hours.

29 Mr Khan gets paid 50c for each unit he completes up to 80 per day, and then 60c for every unit he completes above 80. In one week, the number of units he completed were:

Mon	Tues	Wed	Thurs	Fri
240	212	254	275	235

   a How many units did he complete in the week?

   b For how many of these is he paid at the lower rate?

   c Work out his gross earnings for the week.

30 Amelia is paid a basic wage of $300 a week plus a commission of 2% on all sales over $40 000. Work out Amelia's gross pay for a week when she sells goods worth $55 000.

31 Zane is paid $3.00 for each article he completes. For every article completed above 20 each day, he is paid $3.20.

   a On Monday, Zane completes 30 articles. How much does he earn on Monday?

   b This table gives Zane's production figures for the rest of the week.

Tues	Wed	Thurs	Fri
25	27	19	32

Find Zane's gross earnings for the whole week.

Use the exchange rates in this table for questions **32** and **33**.

US$	UK£	Barbadian$	Canadian$	Trinidad$	Jamaican$
1	0.76	2	1.29	6.7	130

32 Convert:

   a US$50 into Trinidad dollars _____

   b US$550 into Barbadian dollars _____

   c US$70.45 into Jamaican dollars _____

   d US$230 into UK pounds. _____

33 Giving your answers correct to the nearest cent, convert:

   a Trinidad$500 into US$ _____

   b Trinidad$2000 into UK pounds _____

   c Jamaican$10 000 into Barbadian$ _____

   d Canadian$800 into Jamaican$. _____

34 Work out the quarterly telephone bill for Mrs Walcott if she used 946 units at 9.5c per unit and there is a standing charge of $44 per quarter.

35 Natori pays $20 a month for her cell phone on a contract lasting two years. How much does she spend on her cell phone over these two years?

36 Mr Farah's landline costs him $90 per quarter plus a charge of 21c for each unit used. Calculate Mr Farah's bill for a quarter in which he uses 5136 units.

37 Jason buys a sim free cell phone for $1450. He enters a contract for a sim card that costs him $15 a month. The contract gives him a free allowance of 250 minutes of calls, 500 texts and 1GB of data. For each minute he exceeds his free calls he is charged $0.50, for each text over his allowance he is charged $0.25, and for each GB over his allowance he is charged $10.
Find his bill for a month in which he uses 420 minutes on calls, sends 580 texts and uses 1.6 GB of data.

38 How many kilowatt-hours (i.e. units) will each of these appliances use in 1 hour?

   a a 60 W bulb _____

   b a 2 kW electric fire _____

   c a 25 W radio _____

   d a 100 W food mixer _____

   e a 900 W toaster _____

39 How many units of electricity would:

   a a 12 W bulb use in 50 hours

   b a 200 W refrigerator use in 24 hours

   c a 3 kW heater use in 8 hours

   d a 1.8 kW iron use in $1\frac{1}{2}$ hours?

40 Last quarter Mrs Joseph used 954 units of electricity. Each unit costs 14c and there is a standing charge of $35 per quarter.

   a Calculate Mrs Joseph's electricity bill for the quarter (i.e. 13 weeks).

   b How much is this per week?

41 The meter reading on Mr Khan's electricity meter at the end of the first quarter of 2018 was 37899. His meter reading at the end of the second quarter of 2018 was 38045.

   a How many kWh did Mr Khan use in the second quarter?

   b Mr Khan's charges are 67.3c per kWh used together with a fixed charge of $38.50. Calculate Mr Khan's electricity bill for the second quarter.

42 In one quarter Miss James used 350 basic units of electricity at a cost of 20c per unit and 180 units of off-peak electricity at a cost of 15c per unit. She also pays a fixed charge of $60 each quarter. Calculate Miss James' electricity bill for this quarter.

43 Calculate the quarterly electricity bill for Mrs Peters during which she used 760 basic units and 502 off-peak units. Basic units cost 15.2c per unit. Off-peak units cost 8.9c per unit. The fixed charge is $82 per quarter.

1

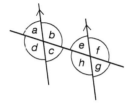

Write the letter of the angle that corresponds to the angle marked.

c _____

b _____

a _____

h _____

2

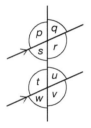

Write the letter of the angle that corresponds to the angle marked.

v _____

q _____

p _____

w _____

In questions **3** to **6**, write the size of the angle marked *d*.

3

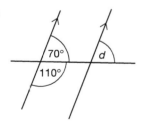

d _____

4

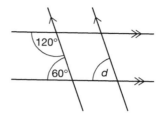

d _____

5

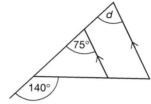

d _____

6

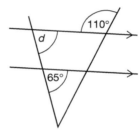

d _____

In questions **7** to **14**, find the size of each marked angle.

7

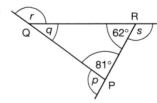

p _____

q _____

r _____

s _____

8

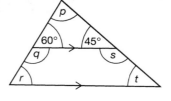

p _____

q _____

r _____

s _____

t _____

9

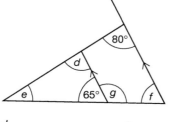

d _____   e _____

f _____   g _____

10

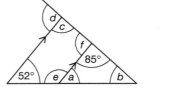

a _____   b _____

c _____   d _____

e _____   f _____

11

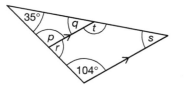

p _____   q _____

r _____   s _____

t _____

12

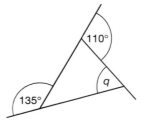

q _____

13

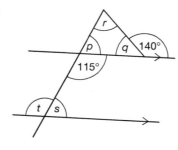

p _____

q _____

r _____

s _____

t _____

14

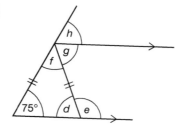

d _____

e _____

f _____

g _____

h _____

15

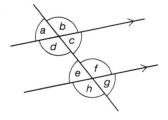

Write the letter of the angle that is alternate to the angle marked.

e _____

f _____

16

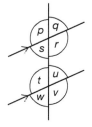

Write the letter of the angle that is alternate to the angle marked.

s _____

t _____

In questions **17** to **24**, find the size of each marked angle.

17

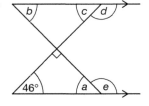

a _____

b _____

c _____

d _____

e _____

18

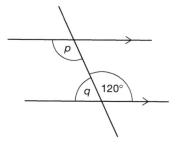

p _____

q _____

19

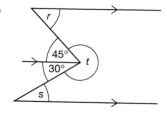

r _____

s _____

t _____

20

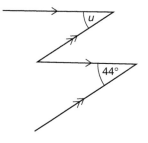

u _____

21

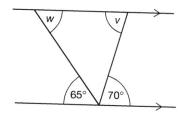

v _____

w _____

22

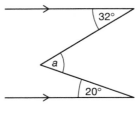

a _____

23

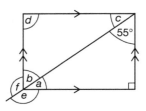

a _____

b _____

c _____

d _____

e _____

f _____

24

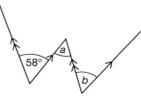

a _____

b _____

25

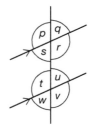

Write the letter of the angle that is interior to the angle marked.

s _____

u _____

In questions **26** to **37**, find the size of each marked angle.

26

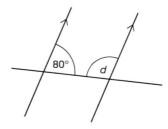

d _____

27

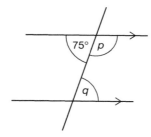

p _____

q _____

28

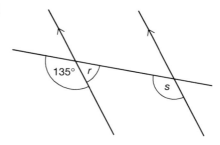

r _____

s _____

29

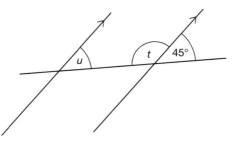

t _____

u _____

30

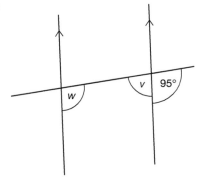

v _____

w _____

31

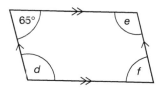

d _____

e _____

f _____

32

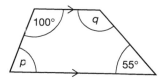

p _____

q _____

33

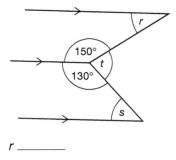

r _____

s _____

t _____

34

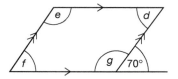

d _____   e _____

f _____   g _____

35

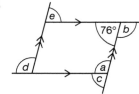

a _____   b _____

c _____   d _____

e _____

36

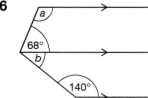

a _____

b _____

37

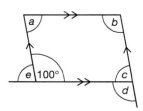

a _____

b _____

c _____

d _____

e _____

38 Which of the following figures are regular polygons? Give a reason for your answer.

a parallelogram

_____

b equilateral triangle

_____

c rectangle

_____

39 Name these shapes. Which, if any, shapes are regular?

_____   _____

_____   _____

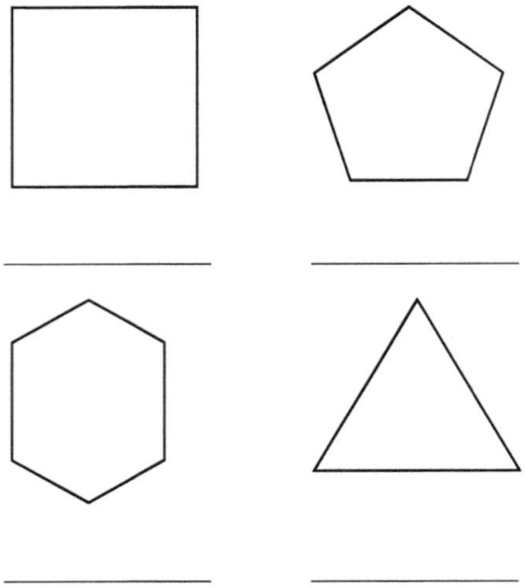

40 Name these shapes. Which, if any, shapes are regular?

_____   _____

_____   _____

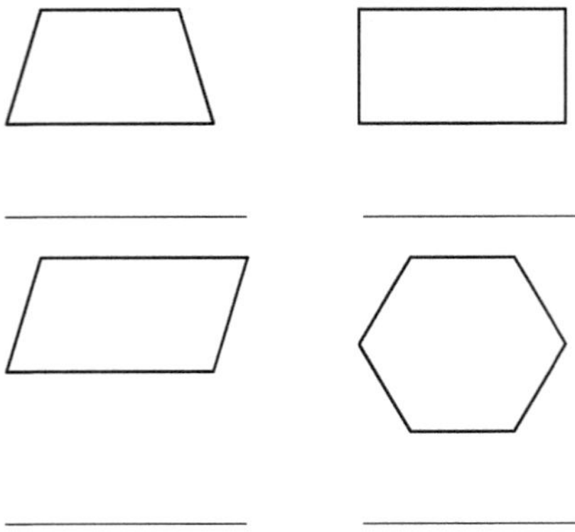

41

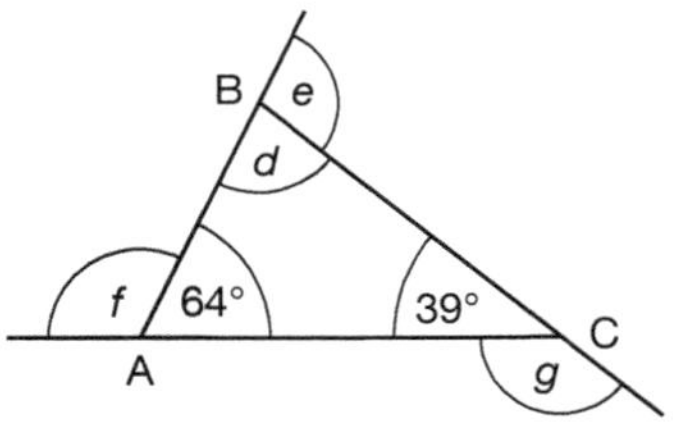

In triangle ABC find:

a the size of each marked angle

_____

b the sum of the exterior angles.

_____

42

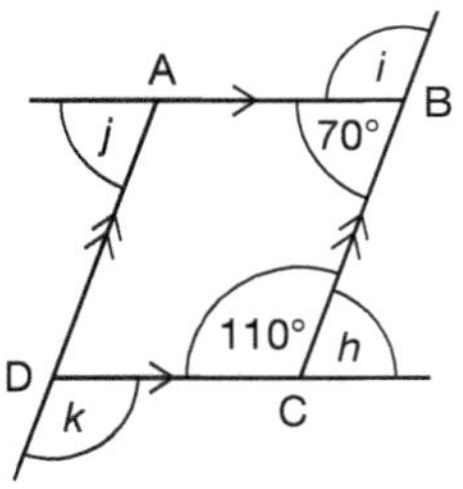

ABCD is a parallelogram. Find:

a the size of each marked angle

_____

b the sum of the exterior angles.

_____

In questions **43** to **48**, find the size of each of the marked angles.

43

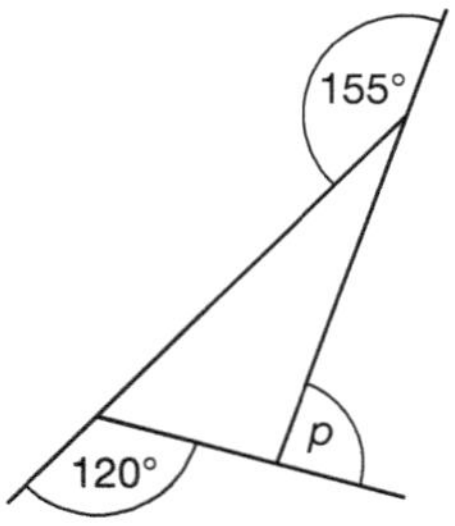

_p_ _____

44

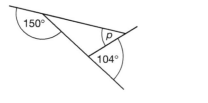

p _____

45

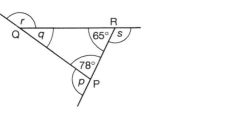

p _____

q _____

r _____

s _____

46

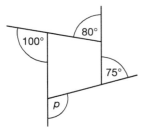

p _____

47

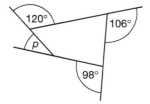

p _____

48

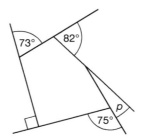

p _____

49 Find the value of x.

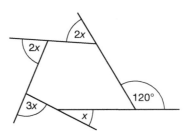

_____

50 How many sides does a polygon have if each exterior angle is:

a 45°

_____

b 15°

_____

c 12°?

_____

51 Is it possible for each exterior angle of a regular polygon to be:

a 60°

_____

b 50°

_____

c 36°?

_____

52 ABCDEF is a regular hexagon.
O is equidistant from all the vertices.

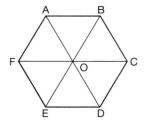

Find:

a the size of each angle at O

_____

b the size of each angle in triangle ABO.

_____

53 ABCDEF is a regular hexagon. O is equidistant from all the vertices.

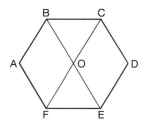

Find:

a the size of each angle in triangle OBC

_____

_____

_____

b the size of angle BAF.

_____

54 ABCDEF is a regular hexagon. AB and DC are produced to meet at P.

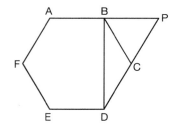

Find the size of each of the angles in triangle BPD.

_____

_____

_____

15　Constructions

Before you start a construction, remember to make a rough sketch and the put all the information that you have on to that sketch. Then decide how to use it.

Construct the following shapes using only a ruler and a pair of compasses.
If you need more space than that provided, use an extra piece of paper.

1

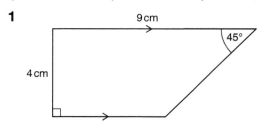

2

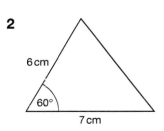

3

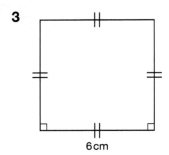

6 cm

4

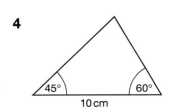

45°   60°
10 cm

5

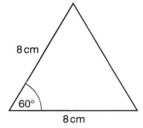

6

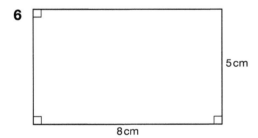

7

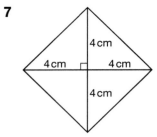

8

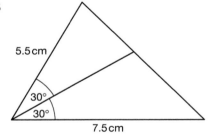

For the remaining questions use only a ruler and a pair of compasses.

9 **a** Construct a triangle ABC, in which AB = 9.5 cm, AC = 4.5 cm and BC = 7 cm.

b Construct the perpendicular from C to AB.

c Measure and record its length.

10 **a** Construct the isosceles triangle PQR in which PQ = 7 cm, PR = RQ = 5 cm.

b Construct the perpendicular bisector of the side PQ.

c Explain why this is a line of symmetry of triangle PQR.

11 **a** Construct the isosceles triangle ABC, in which AB = 4 cm, AC = BC = 7 cm.

    b Construct the perpendicular bisector of the side AC.

    c This line is not a line of symmetry of triangle ABC. Why not? _____

12 **a** Draw a circle of radius 5 cm. Mark its centre C.

    b Next draw a chord PQ about 7 cm long.

    c Now construct the line of symmetry.

13 **a** Construct a triangle XYZ, in which XY = 9 cm, XZ = 8 cm and YZ = 7 cm.

b Construct the perpendicular bisector of XY.

c Construct the perpendicular bisector of YZ.
Where these two perpendicular bisectors intersect, mark C.

d With the point of your compasses on C and with a radius equal to the length of CX, draw a circle.

e Does this circle pass through the other vertices of the triangle? _____

14 Repeat question **13** for triangle XYZ, where XY = 10 cm, angle XYZ = 90° and YZ = 7 cm.
Mark the point G where the two perpendicular bisectors of XY and YZ intersect.
What is special about:

a the point G

_____

b the radius of the circle?

_____

1 The table shows the favourite colours of 36 girls in a class.

Favourite colour	Yellow	Blue	Green	Red
Frequency	4	7	13	12

Draw a pie chart to represent this information.

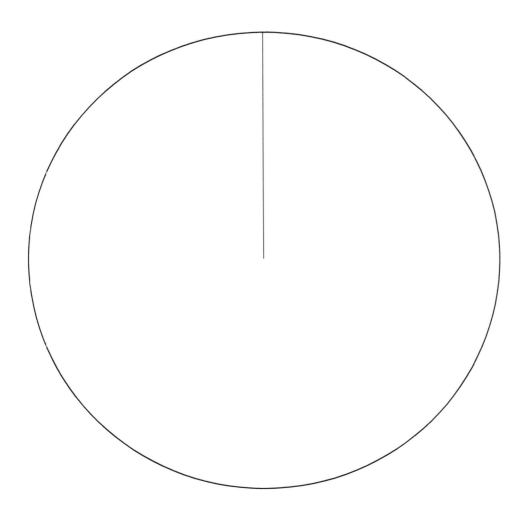

2 Ninety families were asked how they went to the market to do the weekly shop.
The results are given in the table.

Transport	On foot	Car	Bus	Bicycle	Motorcycle
Frequency	22	26	29	8	5

Draw a pie chart to represent this information.

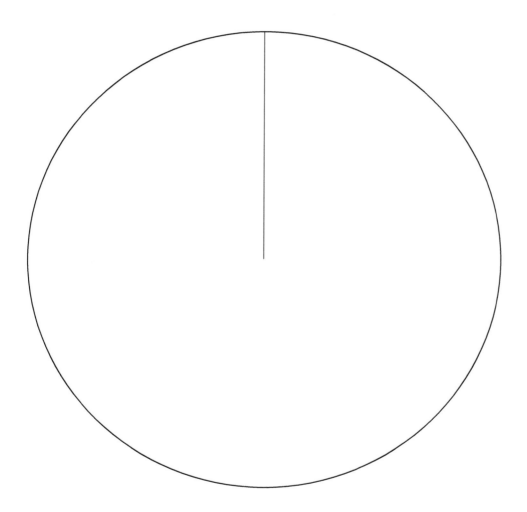

3 St John's fixture list for the season showed that 36 matches had been arranged. Seven were cancelled due to bad weather, 14 produced wins, 8 were lost and the remainder drawn.

a How many matches were drawn?

_____

b Show this information in a table.

c Now draw a pie chart to illustrate it.

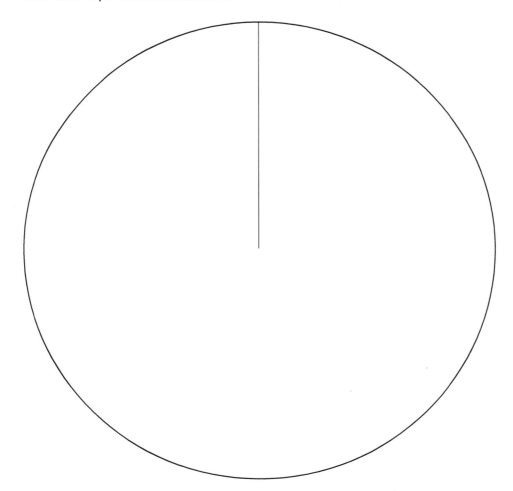

4 Yesterday Laura kept details of how she spent each hour of the day.
The table shows the result.

Activity	Sleep	School	Homework	Leisure	Travel	Meals
Number of hours	8	6	2	5	2	1

Draw a pie chart to illustrate this information.

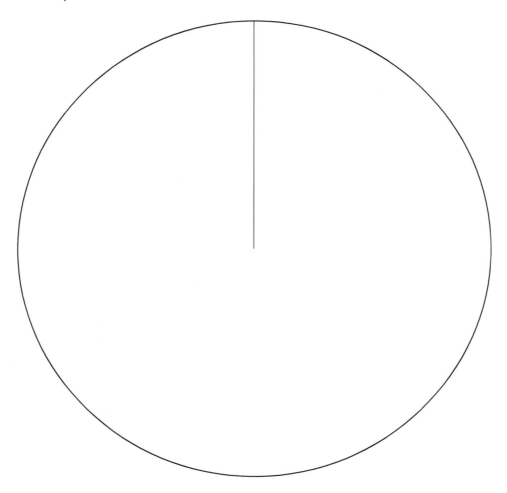

5 The profits from five shops in a chain are shown in the table.

Location of shop	Menton	Northsea	Wayland	Perlo	Benham
Profit ($000)	850	300	1200	1300	300

Draw a pie chart to show this information.

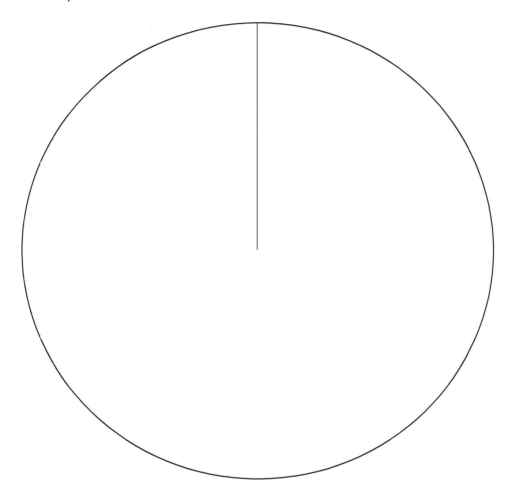

6 360 men, women and youths work at a factory. Use the pie chart to find:

a the number of women working at the factory

_____

b the number of youths working at the factory.

_____

(The angle between the radii drawn to any two adjacent marks
on the circumference is 45°.)

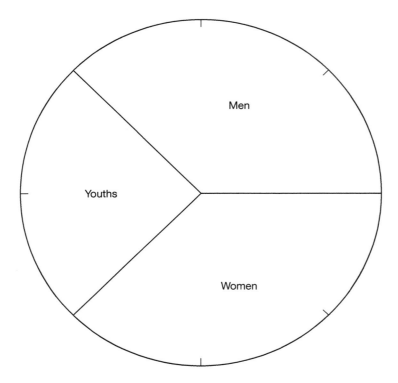

7 This pie chart shows the countries to which Barbados exported during one particular year.

   a Which country was the biggest importer of goods from Barbados?

   _____

   b What percentage, to the nearest whole number, of the exports went to the country that is the answer to **a**.

   _____

   c What percentage, to the nearest whole number, of the exports went to Japan?

   _____

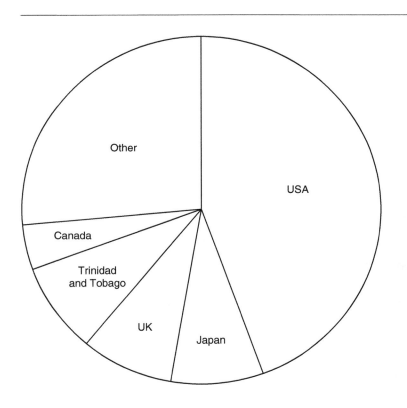

8 120 people were asked to name their favourite fruit.
Their answers are shown in the pie chart.

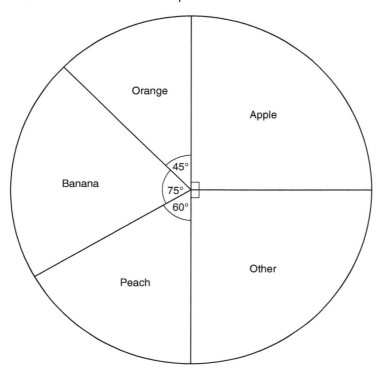

a What fraction chose:

   i an apple   _____

   ii a banana?   _____

b What fraction did not choose an orange or a peach?

   _____

c How many chose:

   i an apple   _____

   ii a peach   _____

   iii an apple or a banana?

   _____

9 1080 adults were weighed and placed into one of four categories:
underweight, average, overweight, obese (i.e. grossly overweight).

The pie chart shows the proportion of adults falling into each category.

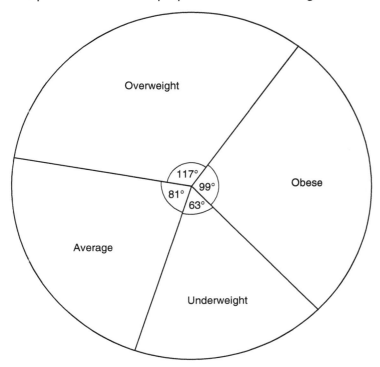

a What fraction of the group were:

   i overweight   _____

   ii obese   _____

   iii above average?   _____

b How many of these adults were:

   i underweight   _____

   ii either above average weight or below average weight?

   _____

c What percentage of the group were:

   i obese   _____

   ii not above average weight?

   _____

10 This pie chart shows the proportion, by mass, of the various nutrients in a packet of oat cereal.

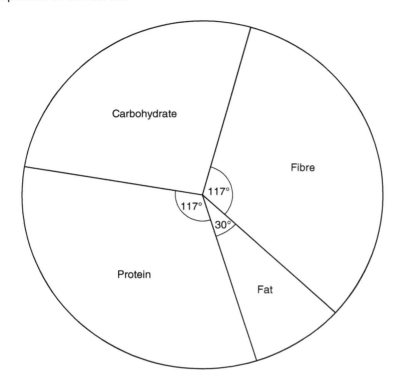

a What fraction of the nutrients is:

   i fat   _____

   ii fibre   _____

   iii carbohydrate?   _____

b How many grams of protein are there in a serving of:

   i 100g   _____

   ii 36g?   _____

c How many grams of carbohydrate are there in a serving of:

   i 100g   _____

   ii 36g?   _____

11 Find the mean, mode and median of each set of numbers:

a 10, 8, 12, 15, 14, 13, 12

   i Mean   _____

   ii Mode   _____

   iii Median _____

b 1.4, 1.8, 1.7, 1.2, 1.2, 1.3, 1.2

   i Mean   _____

   ii Mode   _____

   iii Median _____

c 2.8, 1.7, 2.7, 2.5, 3.1, 2.9, 3.4, 2.1

   i Mean   _____

   ii Mode   _____

   iii Median _____

12 A school entered eight girls in a swimming competition. The marks they scored were:

    72, 95, 85, 43, 75, 82, 63, 59

Find:

a the mean mark _____

b the median mark _____

c Does the mean or median give the best representation of the group as a whole? (Briefly say why.)

_____

_____

13 Stuart counted the number of letters in the words in a paragraph of a book he was reading. They were:

    2 5 7 5 2 8 8 7 6 3

    4 7 6 12 1 7 13 9 9 8

    5 9 4 6 6 9 3 10 12 7

How many words were there in the paragraph?

_____

For the data find:

a the mean number of letters per word

_____

b the mode

_____

c the median.

_____

14 The numbers of goals scored by a soccer team in the last eight matches of the season were 1, 0, 2, 1, 3, 7, 1 and 5. Find the mean, mode and median of the number of goals scored.

a mean   _____

b mode   _____

c median _____

15 The mean of 12 numbers is 6.5. What is their sum?

_____

16 The mean of 8, 10, x, 13, 14 and 16 is 12. Find the value of x.

_____

17 The mean height of 12 boys in a class is 162 cm. The mean height of 8 girls in the same class is 162 cm. Find:

a the total height of the 12 boys

_____

b the total height of the 8 girls

_____

c the total height of the 20 pupils

_____

d the mean height of the group.

_____

18 The table shows the number of tickets bought per person for a pop concert by the first group of people in a queue.

No. of tickets bought	1	2	3	4	5	6	7
Frequency	300	250	120	45	3	10	2

  a How many people were in the first group to buy tickets?

  _____

  b Find the mean number of tickets bought.

  _____

  c Find the mode.

  _____

19 Four coins were tossed together 40 times and the number of heads per throw was recorded in a table.

No. of heads	0	1	2	3	4
Frequency	3	10	17	8	2

Find:

a the median number of heads per throw

  _____

b the mode

  _____

c the mean.

  _____

20 Dr Ali recorded the number of patients he saw each hour over a period of a week. The data are given in the table.

No. of patients	4	5	6	7	8	9	10
Frequency	5	8	12	8	7	3	4

  a How many patients did he see?

  _____

  b For the data find:

    i the median

  _____

    ii the mode

  _____

    iii the mean.

  _____

21 A gymnastics competition was marked out of 40. The marks scored by the competitors were as follows:

12	23	31	18	29
23	34	14	23	35
18	27	16	15	14
16	15	25	36	18

  a How many competitors were there?

  b Write:

    i the highest mark   _____

    ii the lowest mark.   _____

  c Find the median mark.   _____

  d Calculate the mean mark. _____

22 One morning Dave watches his fellow workmates arriving by car as they enter the car park. He counts the number of occupants in each car and obtains the following list:

1, 2, 2, 2, 1, 1, 4, 3, 2, 1, 2, 1, 1, 5, 2, 1, 2, 3, 1, 1

a How many cars are there in the survey?

b How many workmates does he count altogether?

c What is the mean number of occupants per car?

d What is the modal number of occupants per car?

e What is the median number of occupants per car?

23 Over the space of one year the days off sick taken by the staff in a shop were:

4, 23, 0, 1, 0, 10, 0, 3, 18, 35

a How many staff are employed at the shop?

b Find the total number of days lost.

c Find:

   i the mean

   ii the mode

   iii the median.

24 Some of the patients who attend a doctor's surgery one morning have their diastolic blood pressure taken. The diastolic pressures recorded, in millimetres of mercury, were:

82, 88, 69, 76, 84, 90, 75, 62, 80, 84, 93, 79, 88

a How many patients have their blood pressure taken?

b Find, correct to the nearest whole number, the mean diastolic pressure for the group.

c What is the modal diastolic pressure?

d What percentage of the group have a diastolic pressure greater than 80?

e Find the median diastolic pressure.

25 Pirie was admitted to hospital as an emergency. Her temperature was taken at four-hourly intervals and a record kept on a chart. The chart is shown below.

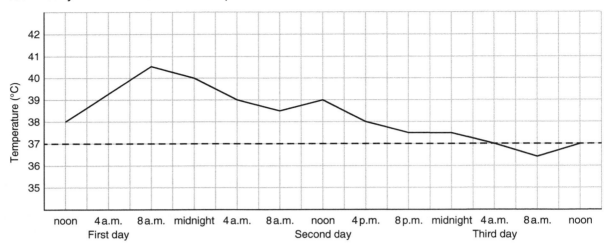

a What was Pirie's lowest temperature?

_____

b Was her highest recorded temperature necessarily her highest temperature? Give a reason for your answer.

_____

c By the third day Pirie was feeling much better. What do you think the dashed line represents?

_____

26 Simon measured the height of a plant at the end of each week for eight weeks. His values are shown on the graph.

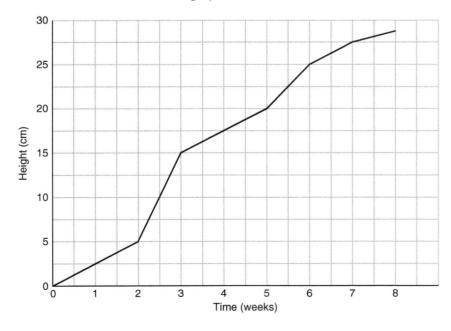

a How high was the plant after:

    i 2 weeks _____

    ii 3 weeks? _____

b How much did the plant grow:

    i in the third week _____

    ii from the end of the 2nd week to the end of the 7th week? _____

c During which week did the plant grow

    i most _____

    ii least? _____

27 This line graph shows the quarterly sales for a manufacturing company.

a What were the first-quarter sales in:

    i 2015 _____   **ii** 2017? _____

b What were the third-quarter sales in:

    i 2014 _____   **ii** 2016? _____

c Find the difference between the second-quarter sales and the fourth-quarter sales in:

    i 2014 _____   **ii** 2017 _____

d In which year was there the greatest difference between sales in the poorest quarter and sales in the best quarter?

_____

e Is there a sales pattern in these figures? If you were the boss would you be satisfied?

_____

f Can you think of a product that would give a sales pattern like this?

_____

g Sketch similar graphs for:

   i an ice cream seller at a seaside resort

   ii the sales of a company distributing school and college textbooks

   iii the sales of sugar in a supermarket.

28 In a survey, the times were taken for a group of students to get to school. The histogram shows the results.

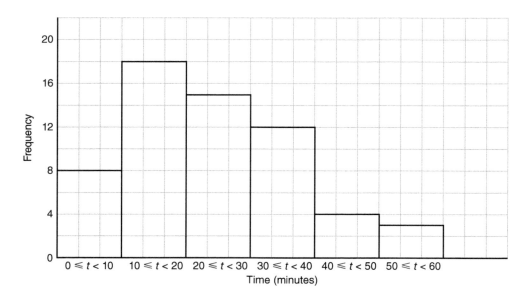

a How many times were recorded?

_____

b Create a frequency table from the details given in the histogram.

c In which group would a time of 20.4 minutes be placed?

_____

d How would you reply if asked to give the shortest time for a student to get to school?

_____

e Estimate the number of times that were more than 25 minutes.

_____

29 The table shows the distribution of the ages of 100 people attending a concert.

Age (t years)	$0 \leqslant t < 20$	$20 \leqslant t < 40$	$40 \leqslant t < 60$	$60 \leqslant t < 80$	$80 \leqslant t < 100$
Frequency	54	20	14	8	4

a Draw a histogram to represent the data given in this frequency table.

b How many people attending the concert were under 40?

_____

c Can you say exactly how many people had been alive for more than 39 years?

_____

d How many people were aged more than 40 but had not yet had their 80th birthday?

_____

In questions **30** to **38**, choose the letter that gives the correct answer.

30 Which of these types of data is discrete?

A Your weight.

B The time it takes you to get to school.

C The number of brothers you have.

D The volume of liquid in your first drink of the day.

31 Which of these types of data is continuous?

A Your shoe size.

B The number of words on a page of this book.

C The score on a die.

D The temperature in school at noon.

32 The mean of the eight numbers 3, 6, 8, 2, 7, 5, 8, 9 is:

A 9   **B** 3   **C** 8   **D** 6

33 The median of the nine numbers 3, 6, 8, 4, 2, 7, 5, 8, 9 is:

A 2   **B** 6   **C** 7   **D** 5

34 The mode of 3, 6, 8, 4, 2, 7, 5, 8, 9 is:

A 5   **B** 6   **C** 7   **D** 8

35 The mean of seven decimal numbers is 5.4. What is their sum?

A 36.8   **B** 37.2   **C** 37.8   **D** 38.4

36 Jen asks 72 of her friends and classmates to choose their favourite colour from red, orange, yellow, green, blue. Eighteen choose red. When she shows her results on a pie chart, the angle she should draw at the centre of the circle to represent red should be:

A 18°   **B** 45°   **C** 90°   **D** none of these

37 For the data given in question **36** the corresponding angle for 'yellow' is 105°. The number who chose yellow was:

A 18   **B** 19   **C** 21   **D** 25

38 This pie chart shows the eye colours of 60 pupils in a school.

Look at the following statements:

i More pupils have brown eyes than green eyes.

ii More pupils have brown eyes than any other colour.

iii More pupils have blue eyes than the other three colours put together.

iv Half the pupils have either green eyes or brown eyes.

Which statements are true?

A **i** and **ii**   **B** **ii** and **iii**

C **ii** and **iv**   **D** **i** and **iv**

39 Give some possible values for:

a the number of people in a minibus

_____

b a person's height

_____

c the world long jump record

_____

d the number of buses at a bus station.

_____

Can each of these values be exact or can they only be given correct to a certain number of significant figures?

1 Give the following ratios in their simplest form:

   a 24:16   _____

   b 64:72   _____

   c $\frac{1}{6}:\frac{2}{3}:\frac{1}{2}$ _____

   d 81:54:135   _____

   e $3\frac{2}{3}:5\frac{1}{2}$ _____

2 Which is the larger ratio?

   a 20:7 or 23:8   _____

   b 3:11 or 5:22   _____

3 Express the following ratios in the form $n:1$ giving n correct to 3 s.f. where necessary:

   a 5:4   _____

   b 10:3   _____

   c 6:7   _____

4 Find the ratio of the following prices:

   a 84c for 12 to 8c each   _____

   b 50c per kg to $400 per tonne

   _____

   c $27 per metre to 36c per cm.

   _____

5 A rectangle is 12 cm long and 8 cm wide. A second rectangle is 8 cm long and 5 cm wide. Find the ratio of their:

   a lengths   _____

   b widths   _____

   c perimeters   _____

   d areas.   _____

6 Find the value of x if:

   a $x:3 = 5:4$ _____

   b $x:6 = 3:7$ _____

   c $4:x = 2:5$ _____

   d $5:6 = x:2$ _____

7 The ratio of the number of girls to the number of boys in a class is 7:5. There are 15 boys. How many girls are there?

_____

8 a Divide $56 into two parts in the ratio 5:2.

_____

   b Divide 135 m into three parts in the ratio 1:3:5.

_____

   c Divide 1 hour 17 minutes into three parts in the ratio 2:3:6.

_____

9 One litre of fuel takes a car 22 km. At the same rate, how far does this car travel on:

   a 4 litres   _____

   b 5.6 litres?   _____

10 The cost of 1 kg of mixed vegetables is $2.64. Find the cost of 34 kg.

_____

11 Six cups and saucers cost $19.20. What is the cost of one cup and saucer?

_____

12 The cost of running an electric fan for 4.5 hours is $2.34. What is the cost of running the fan for 1 hour?

_____

13 A machine uses six units of electricity in four hours. How many units does it use in five hours?

_____

14 A ½ kg bag of sweets cost $6. At the same rate what would a 1¾ kg bag cost?

_____

15 Pamela changed EC$55 into US dollars and got $25 for them. How many US dollars would she get for EC$616?

_____

16 It cost $1320 for tickets for a group of 12 students to attend a concert. How much would it cost for tickets for 19 students?

_____

17 An 8 kg bag of potatoes cost $33.60. At the same rate, what would a 50 kg bag cost?

_____

18 A school allows 95 exercise books a year for every 5 students. How many exercise books are needed for 24 students for a year?

_____

19 a An athlete runs at 8 m/s. How long does it take him to cover 400 m?

_____

b A liner cruises at 26 nautical miles per hour. How long will it take to travel 3536 nautical miles?

_____

20 Find:

a the average speed in km/hour for a journey of 50 km in 30 minutes.

_____

b the average speed in mph for a journey of 4 miles in 40 minutes.

_____

21 A recipe for Chinese bean sprouts to serve four lists these ingredients:

50 g chicken	20 ml peanut oil
4 spring onions	500 g bean sprouts
root ginger	80 ml chicken stock
4 celery sticks	10 ml soy sauce
100 g mushrooms.	

a How much will the peanut oil cost if it is sold in litre bottles at $20 each?

_____

b How much will the chicken cost at $22.40 per kg?

_____

c A bottle of soy sauce contains 150 ml. How many servings of Chinese bean sprouts should this bottle be sufficient for?

_____

d List the ingredients to serve 10 people.

_____

_____

_____

22 Kevin buys enough turf to lay a rectangular lawn measuring 36 m by 24 m. He changes his mind and decides that his rectangular lawn will be 32 m long. If he lays all the turf how wide is it?

23 A short story has 121 lines with an average of 15 words per line. It is retyped with an average of 11 words per line. How many lines will there be?

24 A spreadsheet containing the results of a survey has 34 rows with 12 cells in each row. The same results can be entered in the same number of cells but with 24 rows. How many cells are needed in each row?

25 In a factory, 63 machines are needed to produce the required number of units in 48 hours. How many machines are needed to produce the same number of units in 42 hours?

26 In a large company, 30 offices are needed if there are 8 people in each office. How many offices would be needed if there were 10 people in each office?

27 A book is 156 pages long if the text is arranged with 39 lines to each page. How many pages will be required if the text is reset with the same size type but with 36 lines to a page?

28 Complete the following bill:

	$
5 oranges at 60c each	
3 litres milk at $2.40 a litre	
2 jars of jam at $4.25 per jar	
1 packet of Jello at $2.75	
Total	

29 A salesman receives a basic wage of $75 per week plus commission at 5% of the value of the goods he sells. Find his income in a week when sales amount to $9600.

30 A washing machine is marked $850 plus sales tax at 15%. How much will I have to pay for it?

31 Last month, Rohan saw a computer marked $945 plus sales tax at 15%.

a How much would the computer cost him?

b When he eventually decided to buy, the price of the computer had gone down by $50 but sales tax had gone up to 20%. How much more (or less) did Rohan have to pay?

32 A pack of garden equipment is for sale at $2050. If bought on terms, a deposit of $\frac{1}{5}$ is required, followed by 24 monthly payments of $131. How much is saved by paying cash?

33 A silver medal increases in value by 10% each year. If it is bought for $400 what should it be worth in 3 years' time? (Give the answer correct to the nearest $10.)

_____

34 The table gives the equivalent of US$1 in three other currencies.

US$	UK£	Barbadian $	Canadian $
1	0.80	2.1	1.30

Use this table to convert:

a US$450 to Canadian dollars

_____

b US$500 to Barbadian dollars

_____

c US$950 to UK pounds

_____

d £300 to Barbadian dollars

_____

e 700 Canadian dollars to Barbadian dollars.

_____

35 Find the size of each marked angle.

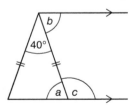

a _____

b _____

c _____

For questions **36** to **47**, you should carry out these constructions outside of your workbook.

Before you start a construction, remember to make a rough sketch and to put all the information that you have on to that sketch. Then decide how to use it.

36 Construct △ABC in which AC = 10 cm, AB = 8 cm and BC = 6 cm.

37 Construct △PQR in which PR = 8.6 cm, $\hat{P}$ = 40° and $\hat{R}$ = 55°.

38 Construct △DEF in which DE = 5 cm, $\hat{D}$ = 35° and $\hat{E}$ = 120°.

In questions **39** to **47**, construct the given figure using only a ruler and compasses.

39

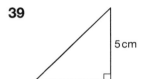

40

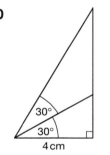

41

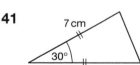

42 Draw a line AB 10 cm long. Construct an angle of 30° at A. Construct an angle of 60° at B. Label C, the point where the arms of angles A and B cross. What should the size of angle C be? Measure $\hat{C}$ as a check.

_____

43 Construct a square of side 7 cm. Draw the diagonals of this square. Measure and record the length of one of these diagonals.

_____

44 Construct △ABC in which AC = 9 cm, AB = 8 cm and BC = 6 cm. Drop the perpendicular from B to AC. Measure and record its length.

_____

45 Construct △XYZ in which XY = YZ = 7 cm and XZ = 6 cm. Construct the bisector of XŶZ and mark W, the point where it cuts XZ. Measure XW and WZ. What special point is W?

_____

46 Construct the isosceles triangle PQR in which PR = 7 cm and PQ = QR = 8 cm. Construct the perpendicular bisector of QR. Explain why this line is not a line of symmetry of PQR.

_____

47 Construct △ABC in which AB = 7 cm, BC = 9 cm and AC = 8 cm. Construct the perpendicular bisector of AB and the perpendicular bisector of BC. Mark E, the point where these two bisectors cross. Draw a circle with its centre at E and radius equal to the distance EA. This circle should pass through B and C. Measure and record its radius.

_____

48 Viv watches his fellow workmates arriving by car to work. He counts the number of occupants in each car and obtains the following list:

1,2,2,2,1,1,4,3,2,1,2,1,1,5,2,1,2,3,1,1.

a How many cars are there in the survey?

_____

b How many occupants does he count altogether?

_____

c What is the mean number of occupants per car?

_____

d What is the modal number of occupants per car?

_____

e What is the median number of occupants per car?

_____

49 The table shows the number of items sold to customers at a till in a supermarket.

No. of items	1	2	3	4
Frequency	8	14	1	9

No. of items	5	6	7	8
Frequency	6	8	9	5

Find:

a the number of customers

_____

b the total number of items sold

_____

c the mode

_____

d the mean

_____

e the median number of items sold.

_____

Great Clarendon Street, Oxford, OX2 6DP, United Kingdom

Oxford University Press is a department of the University of Oxford.
It furthers the University's objective of excellence in research, scholarship,
and education by publishing worldwide. Oxford is a registered trade mark of
Oxford University Press in the UK and in certain other countries

First published by Nelson Thornes Ltd in 2012
This edition published by Oxford University Press in 2020

British Library Cataloguing in Publication Data
Data available

978-0-19-842656-1

10 9 8 7 6 5 4 3 2 1

Printed and bound by CPI Group (UK) Ltd, Croydon, CR0 4YY

Acknowledgements

The publishers would like to thank the following for permissions to use
their photographs:

Cover image: Radachynskyi/iStock

p57: Jason Winter/Shutterstock

Although we have made every effort to trace and contact all
copyright holders before publication this has not been possible in all
cases. If notified, the publisher will rectify any errors or omissions at
the earliest opportunity.

Links to third party websites are provided by Oxford in good faith
and for information only. Oxford disclaims any responsibility for
the materials contained in any third party website referenced in
this work.